W9-BTR-414

CREDIT
AFTER
Bankruptcy

A step-by-step action plan to
quick and lasting recovery after
personal bankruptcy

STEPHEN SNYDER

Published by BELLWETHER, LLC.
6520 Wandsworth Circle
Indianapolis, IN 46250-3410 USA

Thank you to Tyndale House Publishers for the use of *Success! The Glenn Bland Method* audio cassette, an abridgement of *Success! The Glenn Bland Method.* Copyright 1972 by Glenn Bland Publshed 1995 by Tyndale House Publishers, Inc. Used by permission of Tyndale House Publishers, Inc. All rights reserved.

Publisher's Cataloging-in-Publication Data
Snyder, Stephen.
    Credit after bankruptcy : a step-by-step action plan to quick and lasting
    recovery after personal bankruptcy. — Indianapolis, Ind. : Bellwether, 1998.

            p.   cm.

ISBN 1-891945-00-9
1. Finance, Personal—United States. 2. Consumer credit—United States.
3. Bankruptcy—United States.

HG3766 .C74   1998   98-84366
332.7' 5— dc21   CIP

Printed in the United States of America

Contents

*"Where there is no vision,
the people perish"*—Proverbs 29:18

Preface

BANKRUPTCY IS A POWERFUL phenomenon. It is both a financial death and a financial rebirth.

Personal bankruptcy has long been seen as a refuge for blue-collar workers, high-school dropouts, and former high-fliers whose fortunes have turned and who are seeking to shelter their luxury assets. That's no longer the case. The average bankrupt debtor is an absolute typical American, right down the middle. Bankruptcy in the 1990s has become the safety net of the middle class.

That's not to say that famous people do not file bankruptcy. They do. In fact, here are a few names you may recognize who have filed bankruptcy in the past:

Thomas Jefferson
Larry King
M.C. Hammer
Francis Ford Coppola
Debbie Reynolds
Kim Basinger
Redd Foxx
Dorothy Hamill
Wayne Newton
Susan Powter
Burt Reynolds
Governor John Connally
Melba Moore
Toni Braxton
Donald Trump
Abe Lincoln

It's not about how much money you make. If you make poor financial decisions over a long period of time, you will be headed for bankruptcy.

I wrote this book to help bankrupt debtors avoid bad financial decisions that threaten to cripple their financial future. It seems a lot of companies are preying on bankrupt debtors. They think they're doing us a favor by financing a used car at 26 percent.

By avoiding these vultures, and making the proper credit decisions, a bankrupt debtor can recover from bankruptcy within months and build a strong foundation for lasting recovery.

Between these pages you will find an easy-to-follow blueprint that will enable you to re-establish the right type of credit, from the best lenders, in the shortest amount of time. Unlike other books that dispense general financial recovery information, this book confronts the specific issues every bankrupt debtor must face after bankruptcy.

The following information was uncovered through six years of trial and error as my wife and I personally uncovered the truth about re-establishing credit after bankruptcy.

This book was designed to be read by people who have already made the decision to file bankruptcy. It's set-up in three parts. The first eleven chapters act like a prerequisite to the second half of the book. Chapters twelve through thirteen focus on personal development issues. And chapters fourteen through thirty deal with specific issues, like financing a car or mortgaging a home. With that in mind, enjoy.

Stephen Snyder
September 1998

1

Our Story

OUR STORY IS TYPICAL of people who file bankruptcy. We lived beyond our means and chose bankruptcy to avoid garnishment.

At a young age we experienced a high income. That income bought all the toys: luxury cars, a 3,500-square-foot home, fine furniture, clothes, travel, dining out regularly, etc.

In December 1991, less than six months after we married, I decided to make a career change. Looking back, it's easy to recognize that we didn't change our lifestyle after my decision to change careers. The lifestyle remained, even when there was no income. Hard to believe, but true. We survived for over a year by simply selling things from around the house. In December 1992 it finally caught up with us. My wife made the decision to file bankruptcy to avoid garnishment against her wages. She advised me to do the same. She wanted a fresh start for us both.

Like most bankrupt debtors, we couldn't afford to file bankruptcy. So our plan was to find an attorney who would work with us on a payment plan and allow us to do as much of the work as possible to lower the cost. Once my wife's bankruptcy paperwork was complete, I would have an example with which to file my own bankruptcy paperwork with the court. Our motive was saving hundreds of dollars. It worked. With a small loan from my parents, Michele's bankruptcy was filed on December 11, 1992. My bankruptcy followed on February 1, 1993. Both were Chapter 7 filings recorded in South Bend, Indiana.

Filing bankruptcy affected us in two ways. We felt relieved that with our "automatic stay" in hand the harassment was finally over. Creditors would leave us alone. But later we experienced frustration with ourselves in decisions we had made that led up to the bankruptcy. We played the blame game with each other. It almost cost us our marriage.

During the 90 days of waiting for our bankruptcy to be discharged, we had a lot of time to think and reflect. We came to the realization that we were not bad people. Our problem stemmed from errors in judgment that we had repeated daily. Our thinking had been wrong.

Before our bankruptcy was discharged we made seven major decisions and put them in writing. They were:

- We would pay cash for everything, and not go into debt or apply for credit ever again.

- We would pay back our bankruptcy debt with interest, even though we had filed Chapter 7.

- We would radically change our spending habits and thinking about the proper use of money.

- We would begin to give away 10% of our gross income each week.

- We would open a savings account and begin saving 10% of our income.

- We would live within our means.

- We would find a home church and get "plugged in."

The decision to pay cash for everything and reject debt was an emotional decision. It didn't last too long. We realized that credit and debt were not our problem. *We* were our problem. I used the following illustration to explain it to my wife, who was opposed to any new credit: "...A gun can kill. A gun can protect. The end result is determined by the person using the gun..." Credit and debt are not our enemies. With new thinking habits and a plan of action, they can be managed properly.

It's now 1998, over five years since our discharge dates. We've been successful in all but one of our goals—our debt is not paid back yet. We're still working on it. Our biggest success has been the peace of mind our new thinking habits concerning our finances has brought us. We are not concerned about next week's bills. We have successfully entered into mainstream credit in a very short time, and we enjoy the peace that comes from sound financial management.

2

Our Qualifications to Write This Book

THERE ARE NUMEROUS SELF-PROCLAIMED gurus out there who want to help you improve a certain aspect of your life. And that's okay, but take the time to understand what makes them qualified for you to listen. Take today's marriage gurus for instance. The July 1998 issue of SELF Magazine published a story on famous authors who give advice on improving marriages. All but one was divorced several times! The article pointed out that one of the most popular marriage gurus, Barbara De Angeles, is on her fifth marriage. And one of her divorces involved Dr. John Grey, the author of *Men are from Mars Women are from Venus.*

It's important to know what a persons qualifications are before listening to their advice. The only qualifications I have are the results of our actions. Results speak louder than words.

- Two weeks after our bankruptcies were discharged we held our first major Visa bank card issued from a bank.

- In less than 60 days after our bankruptcies were discharged we established new accounts with another bank that extended to us: free checking accounts, Visa debit cards, and several bank loans.

- In less than 90 days after my bankruptcy was filed we mortgaged a beautiful home in Indianapolis through a reputable mortgage lender at 10.5% interest.

- Six months after we closed on our mortgage we refinanced it to a 6% adjustable-interest rate, reducing our mortgage payment from $663 to $441 a month.

- In less than three months after our bankruptcies were discharged we leased a brand-new car from a major car manufacturer at 2.9%. Six months later we leased our second brand-new car at a similar interest rate.

- We were pre-approved to receive a credit card from a major department store within a few months after closing our mortgage.

- 18 months after our bankruptcies were discharged we purchased new furniture on credit.

- 11 months after our bankruptcies were discharged we received a small business loan.

- 12 months after our bankruptcies were discharged a private investor invested $15,000 into our new start-up business.

- 13 months after our bankruptcies were discharged a local bank approved us for merchant status—which enabled our new business to accept major bank cards as a form of payment.

- In less than six months after our bankruptcies were discharged we obtained another bank card from a local bank.

- In less than 12 months after our bankruptcies were discharged we received local store credit to purchase a Nikon camera system.

- In less than 14 months after our bankruptcies were discharged we were able to gain cellular telephone service without a security deposit.

- In less than 18 months after our bankruptcies were discharged we established our first brokerage account with one of the top brokerage firms in the country, and automatically received a Visa debit card.

- In less than 12 months after our bankruptcies were discharged our credit limits began increasing automatically.

- In less than 17 months after our bankruptcies were discharged we were approved for our third brand-new car at a normal interest rate. Six months later we were approved for our fourth new car.

- In exactly 24 months after our bankruptcies were discharged we were approved for a $14,000 home equity loan from a local bank at the same interest rate as a person with excellent credit.

- In 13 months after our bankruptcies were discharged we turned a $500 secured bank card from a local bank into an unsecured bank card with a $5,000 credit limit at 9.9% interest. Six months later the limit was raised to $7,000 with just a 4-minute telephone call.

Can you re-establish credit after bankruptcy? Certainly. In fact, it's easier to re-establish credit after a bankruptcy than it is for a person who hasn't filed bankruptcy and has poor credit!

Let our accomplishments inspire you to reach your goals. Our "re-obsession" with credit was out of necessity. We needed a place to live. We needed a car to drive to work. We needed a bank card when traveling.

This book was written to encourage people who have real needs and have been told it can't be done. Or worse yet, you believe that your only option is high-interest finance companies. If all you get out of this book is hope, our objective has been accomplished.

By conducting free seminars around the country we have experienced first-hand what our example has done—it has changed people's lives. Don't underestimate hope. The hope of achievement is one of the greatest riches in life! Our example is proof that all things are possible.

3

Bankruptcy Defined

BANKRUPTCY IS A LEGAL remedy for previous errors in judgment. Our founding fathers were smart enough to realize that there needed to be a "safety net" to catch people who attempted great things and failed, giving them a fresh start.

Bankruptcy represents both death and life. Death, in that bad habits leading up to the bankruptcy should die. Life, in that it gives another chance to take advantage of the opportunity this great country provides.

The goal now is to recognize previous errors in judgment and quickly correct them. Forgive yourself and move on with your life. Stop looking in the rear-view mirror. Look out the windshield and move forward.

4

Why Re-establishing Credit Is Important

THERE ARE A LOT of people telling you to be debt-free. To avoid credit and pay cash for everything. Not to use bank cards. To purchase a used car at a high-interest rate. To wait several years before you can mortgage a home.

These people have valid ideas. But they are dead wrong. They're missing one important ingredient—they probably have never filed bankruptcy. Therefore, they do not have a clue as to what you are going though. To them, adding $1,000 overdraft check protection takes one telephone call. For you and me, it takes time. Even then, we must beg, and persuade our bankers to extend even the smallest amount of unsecured credit.

These people mean well, but if they haven't experienced bankruptcy, they're not qualified to give you advice. Just ignore them for the time being.

We constantly meet people who filed bankruptcy years ago and never attempted to re-establish their credit. They pay cash for everything. When the time comes to purchase a new car or mortgage a home, no lender will extend them credit.

Why? They are good people. It's been years since the bankruptcy. They earn more now than before and even have a nice savings account. But how can a lender extend credit to someone who hasn't proven they are credit-worthy? They can't.

In fact, mortgage lender guidelines dictate you must establish two or three new credit accounts since your discharge. So if you choose to be a cash-only person and wait 10 years to apply for credit, you would be in a similar situation.

You must have a history of paying on time before mainstream credit lenders will extend you credit. A cash-only system provides no track record. It's just that simple.

After meeting hundreds of bankrupt people through our free seminars, we've noticed that a "cash-only" mentality is very common among recent bankrupt debtors. After six months to two years, the emotion seems to wear off and they're ready to try again. But this time, with a new resolve.

What I am asking you to do is buy into a strategy. I call it the 6 Seasons Strategy.

- The first step of this strategy is to make some life-changing decisions in how you handle your finances. Find the problems. Fix them. Then follow a new plan of action.

- The second step is to strategically go into debt using only mainstream credit lenders—no high-interest companies.

- The third step is to commit to paying your bills early or on time. This is key for a strong financial foundation.

- The fourth step is to become debt-free. Learn to live off a percentage of your total income, and use credit as a convenience, not a necessity.

- The fifth step is credit repair. In the beginning, it's not necessary to spend your time and money repairing your credit reports to look perfect. But once you reach this point and you have a little extra money, you may give it some strong consideration.

- The sixth step is optional. I encourage you to consider paying back your bankruptcy debt, even if you filed Chapter 7. My wife and I made this our first decision. In our minds, our bankruptcy debt became a long-term loan.

So you see, just as there are four seasons every year, there are six seasons in a person's life after bankruptcy. Don't let anyone push you into something that they themselves do not understand.

My friend David wouldn't tell his pastor that he filed bankruptcy. Six years had passed living on a cash-only basis and he now wanted to mortgage a home and acquire a new car. His pastor gave him the best advice he had, which was to not go into debt. It was good advice. But not for that season in David's life.

Remember the seasons. They've worked for us.

5

Is Bankruptcy Wrong?

IS FILING BANKRUPTCY WRONG? Yes. For you to believe otherwise would make you a fool. The best decision you can make right now is to come clean and say something like:

> "I realize that what I did was wrong. I alone am responsible for my decision to file bankruptcy. It was no one else's fault but my own. Today I recognize this and accept it as the truth."

How liberating. So many people neglect to accept responsibility for their actions. They experience denial. It's everyone else's fault. The first step to recovery is to take responsibility for your actions. John F. Kennedy did, and he became a great leader because of it. You can do it too.

Are there some circumstances where bankruptcy truly isn't your fault? Probably. But that percentage is so small, that it's not even worth considering. Walk on the wild side and take responsibility. You'll be glad you did.

Once you reach this point, all you need to do is ask forgiveness. Look at the Apostle Paul. He killed Christians, yet was forgiven, and God used him to take His message to the world.

Then there was King David. This guy had an affair, strategically killed his lover's husband, brought a nation to war, lied, was a poor father, and the list goes on. Yet God said he was a man after His own heart. Wow.

The secret to Paul's and David's ability to move on with their life was their ability to accept responsibility for their actions, ask forgiveness, and forgive themselves. They lived in the present, not in the past. Too many people I've met in our seminars go through life after bankruptcy looking through a rear-view mirror. If you were to drive your car looking through the rear-view mirror, how far would you get? Start looking ahead. Forgive yourself, learn from your mistakes, and move on.

We dealt with this issue in a unique way. We look at our bankruptcy debt as a long-term loan to be paid back with interest. Our part of the transaction is to believe it will be done. God's part is to make it happen. Our goal is to pay it back before the year 2000. Looking at it this way freed us from a lot of guilt. Although I am not telling you to pay your bankruptcy debt back, I am asking you to consider it. It's pretty simple when you understand your role.

If you will do the possible, God will do the impossible.

6

Your Choices After Bankruptcy

FILING FOR BANKRUPTCY FOR many people can be a very emotional experience. There are five initial choices a person may consider after filing bankruptcy. They are:

- Pay cash for everything
- Rely on credit repair
- Create a new credit file
- Develop a new identity
- Re-establish new credit

Let's take a look at each one individually.

PAY CASH FOR EVERYTHING .

On the surface this strategy seems the most practical. However, this should not be your first step. If your goal is to build a log cabin in the mountains, live off the wildlife, and cut yourself off from civilization, a cash-only lifestyle is for you. As you will learn in upcoming chapters, re-establishing new credit after bankruptcy is critical to credit in the future. The sooner you start, the faster you can enter into a cash-only strategy if desired. The fact is that lenders want to see if you have learned how to responsibly handle your finances. No re-established credit—no track record. No track record—no credit.

RELY ON CREDIT REPAIR

As a rule, it is too soon to rely on credit repair. It may be necessary to repair one or two accounts, which you can do yourself. There are plenty of books on the subject. If you hire a professional credit-repair company, it can get expensive and take months to see results. In addition, there are no guarantees. Credit-repair companies will not guarantee that their results will remain long-term. The odds are not in your favor to rely on credit repair to allow you to get credit again. Sure, the claims made by these companies are enticing, but it is just too risky at this point.

The best credit-repair people are lawyers. One excellent attorney I've been watching closely for years has been Attorney Jim Dawson. You may reach one of his senior paralegals Monday through Friday at 1-317-915-2466. They charge you a small monthly fee for their services after work is complete. If you can afford their $60 monthly fee this firm is the best. For further reading, go to their web site: *www.bradleyross.org*.

CREATE A NEW CREDIT FILE

This option was most intriguing to me. I even purchased a course for $600 to explain the process. By making changes to your Social Security number you could have a new credit file within 30 days. There are companies that actually sell information and hold seminars on how to do this. My advice is to avoid this at all costs. There are some ethical questions to consider. Not to mention that it will cost you money. There are also no guarantees. And I almost forgot—it's illegal and considered a federal offense.

DEVELOP A NEW IDENTITY

Does a whole new identity seems exciting to you? You've been watching too many movies. You need to ask yourself, "Do I really want to continue running from my problems?" If you do, books have been written on how to create a new identity. As I leafed through some of these books I had a sick feeling in my stomach. I knew this was not something I could do or recommend to anyone. As I later learned, it's also illegal.

RE-ESTABLISH NEW CREDIT

It seems like a contradiction in terms. Like throwing yourself back into the fire, so to speak. Just remember that credit wasn't the cause of your problem. *You* were the cause of your problem. One of the first questions lenders ask is, "Have you re-established credit since your bankruptcy?" They can't lend money to people who do not show a history of financial responsibility on their credit reports. Fortunately, bankruptcy wipes the slate clean. It's a great opportunity to start over. It makes it easy for a lender to look at your credit report and say, "This person has paid on time for 'x' months after bankruptcy."

The secret to rebuilding your credit after bankruptcy is to build new, positive credit references to outweigh the old ones. The more positive references, the better.

WHAT WORKED FOR US

You must first re-establish mainstream credit. Then you must commit to make early or on time payments. After you have a few major bank cards, secured bank loan, new car, and mortgage, then consider using credit only as a convenience. Make it a goal to minimize your debt. This may take several years.

Then begin cleaning up all three of your credit reports. Just don't rely on credit-repair to solve your financial problems. In May 1999, over six years after filing bankruptcy, we began working with a credit-repair attorney. Before signing up for their services, we performed due diligence on the company for over two years. The results have been amazing, but was expensive. It cost us $200 to start then $115 each month.

Use this strategy, and combined with time you will be on the right path very quickly. Remember, as long as the bankruptcy remains on your credit reports you will be limited in what credit you can receive. Just be glad that you can get credit for the necessary things in life.

7

The Five Questions

BEING APPROVED FOR CREDIT after bankruptcy depends on your individual situation. Your individual situation depends on how you answer the following five questions:

1. Have you received your discharge letter?

2. How long has your bankruptcy has been discharged?

3. How have you paid your bills since the bankruptcy?

4. What new credit have you established since the bankruptcy?

5. How much money you can put down?

QUESTION ONE

Re-establishing credit after bankruptcy starts after you receive your discharge letter from the court, not a minute before. With a copy of this letter in hand, many lenders will welcome you with open arms the very day you receive it. Especially bank card companies and car dealers.

QUESTION TWO

The more time you've accumulated since your bankruptcy, the better. Time is important if you're in the market for a mortgage. Everything in the mortgage industry for a bankrupt debtor is based on time. Banks will want many years of perfect credit before they will extend unsecured credit to you again. And in some cases, as long as your bankruptcy still appears on your credit report, certain banks will not extend credit at all.

QUESTION THREE

Most credit lenders are willing to give you a second chance. But, if you neglect to pay your bills on time after a bankruptcy, you'll have a hard time establishing credit with mainstream lenders. You don't have a choice to be late anymore. Late payments may equal a larger down payment, and a higher interest rate.

QUESTION FOUR

Some lenders need you to re-establish credit after bankruptcy. In fact, mortgage guidelines dictate that you must have at least three new lines of credit to qualify for a mortgage. You must give lenders something to work with. Show them new lines of credit. Show them timely payments. Show them mainstream lenders on your credit report. Show them a down payment.

However, not all new credit is good for you. Stay away from: finance companies, high-interest auto loans, rent-to-own, and other high-interest companies. Using a lot of this type of credit will label you. Stick with mainstream lenders.

QUESTION FIVE

Start saving money. You will need to come up with some cash to use as a down payment. Figure $500 to $1,000 on a new car. Maybe more, depending on the car and your situation. Plan at least $100 for a new bank card. More, if you can afford it. And if you want a new home, plan on 3% to 5% of the purchase price. Possibly more if you have less than two years after your discharge.

These are the five major questions any lender will ask you. Sure, there will be more questions. But these are the foundational questions that everything else will be built upon.

8

21 Things You Must Know
After Bankruptcy

THERE ARE CERTAIN THINGS you must know to make your experience after bankruptcy less hectic. Not taking the time to understand and apply these ideas will severely limit your ability to re-establish credit.

PAY BILLS EARLY OR ON TIME

Paying your bills early or on time after bankruptcy is crucial. Let me repeat: *Paying your bills early or on time after bankruptcy is crucial.* This is the first thing mainstream credit lenders look for. After all, it's a pretty good indication if whether you have truly redeemed yourself from previous bad habits. It's your strongest playing card as you apply for credit. It is one of the essential keys to re-establishing new credit after bankruptcy.

Before our bankruptcies, I refused to allow my wife to handle our checkbook, thinking it's a man's job! I finally gave her control, and now I enjoy not having to deal with it. So if you're not good at managing the checkbook, find someone who is.

Understand which bills, if paid late, will not affect you negatively. For us, it was our fitness club membership dues, long distance phone bill, and Internet service provider. As a general rule, if a company reports to the credit bureaus, pay on time. How do you know if they report? Purchase a copy of each of your three credit reports and look.

Falling short now and then may seem normal. But I challenge you to take a serious look at your finances. Falling short is a financial red flag. Where there is smoke there is fire. Quickly determine what is causing this problem, and aim to fix it before it gets out of control.

When you pay your monthly bills, always pay more than the minimum payment due. The Sears Tower in downtown Chicago was probably paid for by people who pay only their minimum payment due. The interest you pay over a period of time is outrageous. My wife and I always pay at least twice the minimum amount due, sometimes even four to six times the amount due. Worst case, at least pay one dollar above the minimum payment due each month.

If you are a minimum-payment person, you really have no business re-establishing credit. Credit lenders are encouraged when they see that you can consistently pay more than what's due each month.

MAINSTREAM VS. HIGH-INTEREST FINANCING

The only credit that you should consider obtaining is what I call "mainstream" credit. This is the type of credit that you are proud to have on your credit report. Finance companies do not qualify as mainstream. Neither does buy-here-pay-here. Or banks, spelled "b-a-n-c." And certainly not rent-to-own. Companies that do not report to the credit bureau are useless. What good is it if you receive mainstream credit and it's not reported to any of the major credit reporting agencies? Then there's the sneaky kind of high-interest finance companies hidden within large retail companies. CompUSA is a national computer reseller with financing programs provided by high-interest financing companies. Not good. Don't give up. A trend is developing among newer retail stores to provide bank financing (spelled b-a-n-k), like Incredible Universe or Best Buy.

So what's the big deal? For starters, high-interest financing is very expensive financing. More important, mainstream financing begets more mainstream financing. High-interest financing begets more high-interest financing.

A student in our very first seminar in April 1995 raised his hand and complained that no one would give him mainstream credit. I asked him about his current credit situation. He proudly explained that his car was financed at 26% and his mortgage was at 21%. His credit cards were well above 21%. His new computer was also with a high-interest finance company. He went on and on. The lesson is that credit lenders consider you a prime high-interest customer if you already have a lot of high-interest credit. Avoid high-interest credit like the plague.

Some examples of high-interest financing:

- Buy-here-pay-here auto companies
- Finance companies
- Rent-to-own companies
- Department store finance programs
- Investor financing for mortgages
- High-interest auto financing through car dealers

It's difficult to turn away from high-interest financing. We were tempted many times. Thank God we didn't do it. We wouldn't be where we are today if we had. Mainstream credit is worth waiting for. It really is. It's the difference between recovering in months or years. The choice is yours.

Pick the companies you do business with just as closely as a movie star would select a movie role. You don't see Harrison Ford starring in B movies. He has a reputation and public image to uphold. Same goes for you with mainstream credit. High-interest financing is tempting, but it will lead you to ruin.

Some examples of mainstream credit:

- Major bank cards issued from a bank
- Secured bank loans (spelled b-a-n-k)
- Car-manufacturer financing
- Reputable mortgage companies

YBFD

You're buying the financing, dummy. That's what YBFD stands for. Sometimes people who file bankruptcy have an attitude. They feel they should be treated like everyone else. Well, yes and no. You need to build up to that. You need to start small and prove that you are financially responsible. Within 12 to

24 months you will regain a portion of the respect you deserve. But to completely recover takes time. Your first credit purchases after bankruptcy are important. Unlike most people who get to shop and make decisions based on what they want, we must "buy the financing."

So what does this mean, exactly? It means you ask the car dealer which car you should be looking at. It means that when shopping for a house you go to a mortgage lender to get pre-approved before you go house-hunting. It means ignoring the high interest rate on your bank card for the first year or so. It should be lowered in the second year, with an excellent payment history. Your whole approach to credit will change for the next 12 to 36 months. Only after you've re-established mainstream credit, created an excellent payment history, and put some distance between you and your bankruptcy will you have more choices.

So many people get this turned around. They want a new car. So they decide exactly which one they want, talk to the salesperson, and take a test drive. Then they get frustrated when they are unable to obtain financing. I would encourage you to remember the YBFD formula. It's really simple. Determine whether you can obtain financing first. Talk with the person who controls the money, not a salesperson.

FILING DATE VS. DISCHARGE

Understand the difference between the date you filed bankruptcy and the date of your discharge. This is important. Everything begins from your discharge date. For example, if a mortgage lender's policy is to extend credit to people with a bankruptcy after two years, what that really means is two years since the discharge date. Memorize your discharge date. If you don't know it, call your attorney or local bankruptcy court and ask for a copy of your discharge letter.

With that in mind, people who file Chapter 13 bankruptcy protection are severely limited in what they can do after filing bankruptcy. Essentially, they must get the approval of a bankruptcy judge through their trustee to acquire any new credit after bankruptcy (which can be done) or wait until they receive their discharge before re-establishing credit.

Chapter 7 bankruptcy debtors, on the other hand, within 90 days after filing, can literally begin re-establishing credit the day of discharge. The discharge letter is an important letter. Lenders will want written proof of your discharge. Make several copies and put them in a safe place.

In fact, it would be a good idea to make two copies of your entire bankruptcy paperwork. One complete set for you and one for lenders to use. Especially if you want a mortgage. Call your attorney or the local bankruptcy court and ask for a copy. Some attorneys will gladly give you a copy. Others will charge you. You will need it sooner or later, so do it now. The longer you wait, the more difficult and expensive it may be to obtain.

CREDIT GUIDELINES

Every lender has credit guidelines. These guidelines are their own rules that need to be met before they extend a loan to someone. Your main objective is to find out as much as you can about these credit guidelines before making application.

This can be difficult, especially when large firms hire telephone operators to take applications over the phone. These innocent people do not know anything about credit guidelines. In fact, usually what they "know" is completely wrong information.

If I had a dollar every time a telephone operator told me something in error, I could retire to the Bahamas.

A recent occurrence comes to mind. I was ready to switch my cellular telephone service from a "pay-as-you-go" plan to a normal credit plan. I never exceeded the $125-a-month cap on the account, but I was tired of paying a premium per minute rate. I felt that I had established an excellent payment record with them over the last six months. So I called customer service. A woman answered and informed me that I must wait until my contract was renewed in 18 months. I begged and pleaded. She insisted I had to wait 18 months.

A few minutes went by. I didn't want to wait 18 months. I called again. I spoke with another woman. This time I received a different answer. She told me to wait six months. I hung up and waited a few more minutes, then called back. A man answered the phone this time. He told me it takes up to 48 hours to determine whether the company would put me into a normal account. I put in my request and waited for his return call. They approved me. The next day I received a new phone, a new number, a lower monthly payment, and a cheaper per-minute rate. The best part was my monthly cellular phone bill was cut in half the following billing cycle.

Remember, you will talk to people who are paid minimum wage for answering a telephone. They usually are not paid for their knowledge to understand the whole operation. They are paid to answer only certain questions. Anything out of the norm, they typically *guess*.

CO-SIGNERS

Avoid lenders who require you to have a co-signer, period. Move on to the next lender. Co-signing is not good. Concentrate on re-establishing your own credit. This will put you on the fast track to re-establishing credit after bankruptcy. Having a co-signer will only slow you down. If a lender asks whether you can find a co-signer, simply respond "No." It's not even an option. If the lender insists that co-signing is the only way you can get financed, kindly thank them for their time, smile, and move on.

CASH IS QUEEN

You will need cash to re-establish credit after bankruptcy. The more cash you have, the more options you will have. It's just that simple. This doesn't mean you need a lot of cash to re-establish credit. But you will need some cash. If you currently don't have any extra cash, you will need to reduce your living expenses and save money beginning today.

LARGE CITY VS. SMALL TOWN

I was born and raised in a very small town. I could count the stoplights on my two hands. There are benefits to small towns. But establishing credit after bankruptcy is not one of them.

We made a decision to move from South Bend, Indiana, to

Indianapolis in February 1993. It was a tough decision. Our entire family was within a 20-minute drive. It became one of the best decisions we've ever made. It's true, the larger the city, the more options you will have. Smaller towns seem to be more rigid and less innovative. There are always exceptions to the rule, but this is an important decision to consider.

What does this mean, exactly? Well, it could mean that an innovative banker is more likely to be located in a larger city than a small town. It could mean the difference in a car dealership that has enough volume of business to convince their underwriters to take a few marginal deals. Or special first-time-home-buyer programs. It could mean a larger Multiple Listing Service. The benefit of a larger MLS is the option of searching on creative financing. Some small towns don't even have an MLS, let alone the ability to search owners willing to be creative. It could mean the difference between obtaining a new small business loan or not. In summary, you will probably have many more options in a larger city. It worked for us.

NEGATIVE PEOPLE

There are plenty of negative people in this world. Even your family can be a source of negativity. But there is a point where you must draw the line.

We needed to distance ourselves from any type of negativity to enable us to move on with our lives. Surround yourself with people who make you feel good when you're around them. People who make you grow. Who encourage and support you.

Mark Twain once said, *"Keep away from people who try to belittle your ambitions. Small people always do that, but the really great make you feel that you, too, can somehow become great."*

People who live mediocre lives expect you to join them in their misery. Have no part of it. Negative people have fleas. If you get too close or stay too long, the fleas will jump out on you. That's good counsel. It's okay to be around negative people for a brief time, but limit this time for your own benefit.

When we first moved to Indianapolis there was a couple who befriended us. A nice young couple with a beautiful little girl just turning two. We had to limit the amount of time we spent with them because of what they said, their actions, and how they thought. The man of the house was a real-life "Homer J. Simpson" who was barely making a living. Conversations with him were intolerable at best. He was always making negative remarks, justifying his own mediocrity. It was too much for me to handle. So we made a decision to severely limit the time we spent with them. It was hard at first. But our peace of mind was restored and our marriage improved.

AGREEMENT

If you have the benefit of being married, you have an opportunity to avoid costly errors in judgment. It's called being in complete agreement on major decisions that affect your family. As the leader of our home, I am responsible to make the final decision. However, I greatly value my wife's input.

We agreed immediately after our bankruptcy filing to always be in agreement on major issues like purchasing a house, borrowing money, starting a business, etc. If we are not in agreement, it isn't meant to be, and we are to move on. This principle led us to our current home, and what a blessing. Our mortgage payment is less than most people pay for rent. In addition, our home was appraised for over $30,000 more than what we paid for it, in less than 24 months after we purchased it.

I would encourage you and your spouse to be in complete agreement on major issues that concern your family.

WOMEN AND THEIR SIXTH SENSE

Women are born with a "sixth sense." My wife told me many times, after meeting someone I intended to do business with, not to do business with him. She said, "...There's just something I feel about him..." If I had listened to her in the early years it would have saved a lot of grief. Men can learn this "sixth sense," but women have it as standard equipment. Learn to take advantage of it, men.

W2 VS. 1099

Credit lenders prefer W2 income over 1099 income. W2 income is when you are employed by a company. 1099 income is generally when you are self-employed or are an independent contractor.

W2 income is easier to verify. It's less work and less paperwork for lenders. Your chances of re-establishing credit will be greatly enhanced if your income can be supported by W2s.

Mortgage lenders generally look at the last two years to qualify you. Most other lenders take a current picture of your financial condition. Each lender is different. An auto dealer may not even check your income. A mortgage company or bank will want everything documented and will usually check all three credit bureaus. A bank card company, if they have time, may simply do a telephone verification of employment.

So if you're intending to start a new business right after bankruptcy, you may want to start part time and eventually move into full time over an extended period. That isn't to say that re-establishing credit after bankruptcy with 1099 income is impossible. It's just a little more demanding. My wife and I were both self-employed while obtaining the majority of our new credit after bankruptcy. It can be done.

THE MAGIC NUMBER "24"

You can be approved for a mortgage at normal interest rates in as little as 24 months after your discharge, and much earlier if you can prove that your bankruptcy was caused by medical reasons.

In order to qualify to use the magic number "24" you must have paid your bills early or on time since the bankruptcy, have income to support your purchase, have re-established mainstream credit since the bankruptcy, have job stability, maintain respectable debt-to-income ratios, and have a down payment.

Even if you don't meet all these qualifications, you can still get a mortgage. But you may be charged a higher interest rate, and in some cases may need to have a larger down payment. If you need help with a down payment, you're a candidate for a first-time home buyer program.

The key to using the magic number "24" is to find an innovative lender. Forget any prejudices you have against certain companies. The fact is, you're looking for a creative person, not a company. You don't do business with a company. You do business with a person.

WHAT DOES THE WORD "NO" MEAN?

Parents will understand this. What does the word "no" mean to children? That's right, absolutely nothing. At times they keep doing what you told them not to do.

As you begin re-establishing bankruptcy you may hear the word "no" a lot. That's okay. Remember your children. Ignore the people who tell you no, and keep going about your business.

"No" means absolutely nothing!

One powerful example of this principle in action was seen when I decided to start a small business shortly after bankruptcy. It was a home-based mail-order business that would depend heavily on customers giving their credit card numbers over the telephone. It was vital to this business to obtain what's called "merchant status." All this means is that my company would have the ability to accept customers' credit card numbers from people as a form of payment, just like at restaurants or stores.

I called every bank in town. I immediately determined that banks frowned on three major issues: (1) mail-order businesses, (2) home-based businesses, and (3) start-up businesses. Rest assured, a previous bankruptcy did not help things. I was up for the challenge.

I decided to meet with the bank that had the best program. And before I began filling out the credit application I asked the bank representative if a previous bankruptcy would be a problem. The woman froze. It was an awkward moment. I still wasn't completely over the fact that I had filed bankruptcy. I still felt like a financial leper. Her first words were something like "...We can't help you..." The meeting was over. I was told "No."

Before I left the bank, I asked two very important questions. I asked, "Where would you go if you were me?" She didn't know. My second question was, "May I speak with your supervisor?"

She agreed, and proceeded to give me his telephone number.

I scheduled an appointment, and with my best suit on I met with the supervisor a few days later. It was a brief meeting. Maybe five minutes. I gave him my business plan, and a two minute pitch, answered a few questions, then left. A few days later he called to request proof that I had obtained a small-business loan a few weeks earlier. I faxed the loan agreement to him. Later that day I was given pre-approval for merchant status over the telephone from the sales representative that told me "no." The final approval by committee took a few weeks. But in the end I was approved.

It was a great thing. My prayer was answered. I was excited. Especially since I knew another business owner with good credit who couldn't get merchant status.

Later I asked the bank supervisor what made him decide to grant me merchant status. He said it was my business plan and the new small-business loan. By the way, the small business loan was for a whopping $2,000.

What does "no" mean? Absolutely nothing.

WHAT IS FAITH?

Faith is the confident assurance that something we want is going to happen. It is the certainty that what we hope for is waiting for us, even though we cannot see it up ahead.

We must have faith. If we will do what is possible, God will do the impossible.

Faith is important. It amazes me how we struggle with circumstances and at times lose our faith.

Yet look at the miracle of the seed. The farmer plants a seed, and over a period of time it produces in abundance many times over the amount of seed that was planted. Amazing. How does that happen? The farmer does the possible. God does the impossible. Do the possible—have faith.

THE POWER OF QUESTIONS

Learn to ask open-ended questions. Let the curiosity of your childhood come back to life. It's a good thing. Open-ended questions like "What would you do if you were me?" or "Do you know anyone who could possibly help me?"

That's how I first learned about Ford Motor Credit. My wife and I were turned down by Toyota Motor Credit for a new 1993 Toyota Corolla. As we were getting ready to leave I asked, "What would you do if you were me?" The lease finance manager said, "Visit the dealership across the street." He proceeded to tell us, "Ford Motor Credit has the best leasing program in the country. If anyone will take you, it will be Ford."

We couldn't believe our ears. That question led to where we needed to be. We weren't excited about driving an American-made car, but remember—you're buying the financing. Ford leased us two new cars at a very low interest rate.

Accept the fact that you don't know everything. Listen to what experienced people have to say. Save time by asking questions. It will help you accomplish your goals a lot faster.

By the way, we leased our third car after bankruptcy from the Toyota dealer that had told us about Ford.

GET PLUGGED IN

There is a big difference in knowing about God and knowing God. Finding a place of worship is important to your spiritual growth. Think of yourself as a tree looking for fertile ground to bury your roots into. This fertile soil will help sustain you during difficult times in the transition into becoming financially responsible.

If you're like most people, walking into a large church can be a scary proposition. In fact, most people come out the same way they came in. This doesn't have to be.

Most churches now have what are called home groups, or cell groups. These are small groups of people within the church that meet on a regular basis. It's an opportunity to meet with other believers, share experiences, and pray for each other. It's like church all over again, just in a smaller, more personal setting. These groups usually meet in church members' homes.

I would encourage you to find a place of worship and get plugged in. If you have a friend who seems to know something you don't know, ask if you could go to church with him or her.

Start there. Visit a few churches and prayerfully consider where God wants you to be. But don't take too long. Get plugged in!

HOW MUCH NEW CREDIT IS ENOUGH?

The answer is: It depends on your goals. If mortgaging a home is in your future, it will take more than a bank card with a $100 credit limit to re-establish credit. My advice won't accommodate everyone. Overall, I encourage people to begin by establishing a:

1. Bank checking and savings accounts
2. Bank debit card
3. A few secured bank cards
4. Secured bank loans
5. New leased car
6. Home mortgage
7. Refinanced mortgage
8. Home equity loan

Concentrate on the necessities, and let time work miracles. As a frame of reference, mortgage guidelines dictate that you will need two or three new credit references since the bankruptcy.

My friend Steve was paying over $700 for rent in Indianapolis. Since my mortgage was $441 each month, I encouraged him to consider home ownership. My idea was to reduce his house payment. Over a period of a few months he picked out some vacant land and decided to build a new home. Application was made. Hopes were high.

Steve is an intelligent guy. He's the number one salesperson at his company. He saves money. He has a stock portfolio and cash nest egg. His bankruptcy was discharged over two years ago. Steve was turned down for that mortgage by two companies.

I saw it coming. My idea was to reduce his mortgage payment, not multiply it by two. I was thinking of a "used" home, not a brand-new one relying on conventional financing. In addition, the only credit he had established since the bankruptcy was a bank card with a small limit and a small bank loan. As it turned out, there were also tax liens since the bankruptcy.

How much credit is enough? It depends on your goals. If I had inquired further as to what he expected in a home, I would have advised him to wait. Anything is possible, but not all things make sense.

Steve has since been approved for an FHA mortgage. His payment will be less than his current rent.

INDIVIDUAL AND JOINT ACCOUNTS

It's important that if you're married you make the extra effort to re-establish credit both as individuals and together.

The exception to this rule is when one spouse has perfect credit and the other has had a bankruptcy. For more information on this, see *"The Ultimate Credit Handbook"* by Gerri Detweiler.

We put our first car after bankruptcy in my wife's name with me as a co-applicant. Our second car was just the opposite. Our third car was in her name. Our fourth car was in my name. We have individual and joint bank loans, checking accounts, and savings accounts. Our home mortgage is in both names. We each have separate and joint bank cards and debit cards.

We wanted to be sure that if one of us ever died, the surviving spouse would have re-established credit as well. It also makes your credit applications much stronger when two credit-active borrowers are responsible for the loan. And let's face it, we need every advantage we can get.

ATTITUDE

Many people with a bankruptcy have an attitude. They feel that people owe them another chance, regardless. One friend of mine obtained a secured bank card with a low limit. He was shopping one day and saw a really nice coat he wanted to purchase. He realized that he was very close to his credit limit. He was declined authorization, since the purchase would put him a few dollars over his credit limit. He told me later that he planned to cancel that account because he felt their policy "sucked."

My point is this: Be thankful for the opportunity to re-establish credit. Lighten up. Maintain an attitude of thankfulness. You don't deserve anything yet. You haven't had time to prove yourself financially responsible. That time will come. Be patient.

I can't tell you enough how your attitude affects other people. Just for fun, try this. Call a car dealership that you know you will never patronize. Ask to speak with the leasing manager. Tell him your situation. Tell him you want a new car. Tell him what type of car you want. Tell him when you want it. Tell him what interest rate you expect. Tell him as much as you can. Then, tell him to tell you if he can help you.

Now, call another car dealership. Ask to talk with the leasing manager. Before he gets on the line, make a decision that this person knows more than you about cars and that you intend to listen more than you talk. Use his first name throughout the conversation. Explain your situation within 15 seconds. Ask him if this is a good time to talk. Ask him if he thinks he could help you. Ask him what he thinks you should do. Allow him to lead the discussion. Say things like "That's interesting" or "I never thought of that" or "Good idea."

Lenders deal with difficult people all the time. A nice person who cares what they have to say is like a breath of fresh air. Don't give lenders an excuse not to go the extra mile for you. Be kind to everyone, and it will return to you multiplied.

WHERE TO OBTAIN A COPY
OF YOUR CREDIT REPORT

It's important to know the condition of your credit reports. There are three different credit reporting agencies. Every city will have a dominant credit-reporting agency. Here in Indianapolis its Equifax. Ask around to find out which bureau is more commonly used in your area. But its important to know what on all three reports. The main telephone numbers to the three major credit reporting agencies are:

Equifax (CSC Credit Services)	(800) 759-5979
TransUnion	(800) 888-4213
Experian (formerly TRW)	(800) 682-7654

You can also look in the Yellow Pages under credit-reporting agencies for local numbers. If you have been turned down within the last 30 to 60 days, it should be free. When you call, be sure to ask if there's a local office where you can pick up your report.

If you have a dispute, the credit-reporting agencies have established telephone numbers to handle disputes directly over the telephone. Ask for this number when you call.

If you want an easier way to purchase all three of your reports without the hassle—call After Bankruptcy Foundation at 1-317-578-7118. Using their form you will speed up the process, pay only $24, and there will not be any negative credit inquiry appearing on your credit reports. You may also email your request for the credit reports form to *maryann@afterbankruptcy.com*.

9

Put Your Financial House in Order

IT SEEMS ODD FOR me to be writing on the topic of putting your financial house in order. Then again, who else is more qualified to advise you that someone who has been where you've been and fully recovered?

The majority of the principles expressed in this chapter originate from my friends Jim Rohn and Glenn Bland. Their books and audiotapes helped me beyond measure. I recommend purchasing anything these men publish.

IT STARTS WITH YOUR MONEY

The philosophy of the rich versus the poor is this: The rich invest their money and spend what is left; the poor spend their money and invest what is left.

Read the last paragraph again. It's the key to understanding how to put your financial house in order. Ignoring it will always leave you in want. Practicing it will propel you as far away from your current situation as you can possibly imagine.

Did you realize that $17 a month invested at 17% will propel you to millionaire status in 40 years? How many $17-a-month expenses can you eliminate each month to start investing in yourself? This is what motivated me. Later, we'll show you how to safely get a 17% return. For now, let's talk about reducing your cost of living; increasing your income; and learning how the rich handle their money.

STEP ONE: CUT LIVING EXPENSES

The first step anyone can take in an unstable financial situation is to immediately cut your living expenses. Take this very seriously. Most of us need to stage an all-out assault on everything that takes away from your income. Stop throwing away money on useless things.

Have you ever noticed that people in dire financial straits seem to have everything? Large-screen televisions, nice furniture, stereo equipment, expensive appliances, satellite dishes, cable television, fancy cars, etc. Here are some ideas for lowering your monthly expenses:

1. Cancel all newspaper subscriptions
2. Cancel all magazine subscriptions
3. Cancel cable television
4. Stop buying clothes that need to be dry-cleaned
5. Find your pets a new home
6. Move to a smaller house or live with family or friends
7. Cook at home
8. If you must eat out, share meals
9. Breakfast food is cheaper than lunch or dinner
10. Drive a simpler car—try trading down
11. Build a simple wardrobe—try jogging suits
12. Reduce your entertainment to videos or the cinema
13. Drop call-waiting and caller ID
14. Get rid of your car phone
15. Stop sending Christmas cards
16. Live on 70% of what you earn
17. Change the way you shop—purchase generic brands
18. Switch to a bank that offers free checking
19. Live closer to where you work
20. Send more letters, instead of phone calls
21. Make fewer long-distance telephone calls
22. Inquire how to eliminate monthly bank fees
23. Sell things you no longer need through a garage sale
24. Return for credit items you haven't used
25. Eliminate soda from your diet—drink water

26.   Avoid ATM machines unless they're from your bank
27.   Instead of FedEx use Priority Mail
28.   Visit the library instead of the bookstore
29.   Don't play the lottery
30.   Give up smoking
31.   Give up drinking
32.   Ask your pastor if there is somewhere you can stay until
      you get your feet back on the ground

STEP TWO: INCREASE INCOME

Now that you have eliminated some of your monthly expenses,
lets look at your income. It could be as simple as getting a higher-
paying job. If you're married, and both self-employed, someone
needs to generate stable income while the other works on
meeting future goals and dreams.

Some friends of ours were facing a financial crisis. After
talking with them it seemed obvious that they had made the same
mistake we made years ago. Both were self-employed, and the
stability of the income was not there. We advised one of them to
seek full-time employment to stabilize their income. Within
weeks their entire life had changed. The husband accepted a
position working fulltime, providing a stable income for his
family while the wife continued in her business. Their dream is
to own a successful franchise, but that is on hold right now as
they prepare a financial foundation and begin saving for their
future.

If you are married, at least one of you needs a stable income to
support the family. If this simple principle is ignored it could
spell disaster.

How do you get a higher-paying job? The first step is to believe
you can get one. The second step is to commit to "going the extra
mile" for your employer. People that work hard, stay late, arrive
early, and always ask for more to do will get noticed very quickly.
For information on this principle, pick up the book *"Think and
Grow Rich"* by Napoleon Hill.

Once you're mental attitude is right, begin asking people
where the higher-paying jobs are. Here in Indianapolis, I know of
two companies that hire for warehouse work and start at $15 an

hour. I found out about these companies by asking. How many people do you talk to each day? Ask the UPS or FedEx person. Call the Chamber of Commerce. Write a letter to the governor or your senator. Ask your pastor. Ask your friends where they work and their advice on finding a higher-paying job. Read the Sunday classifieds in your local newspaper. Read the Sunday classifieds in the nearest metropolitan area. Ask, ask, ask!

Another way is to start work as a temporary, or "temp." This is becoming the way for large companies to screen long-term employees. They hire temporaries and use this time to screen good workers. When they find one, the person is offered a full-time position. Don't overlook the temp positions.

For people with a professional background, it's even more simple. Focus on sales positions. My friend Connelly use to oversee the small-business division for Ameritech here in Indianapolis. He told me he needs to hire sales people this year, and he's having a tough time finding good people. The average sales person in his office made $75,000 last year.

Employ the services of an employment agency, more commonly known as a headhunter. The company hiring you pays the fee. Over half of the best opportunities don't even hit the classified ad section of the Sunday newspaper!

The trick in dealing with headhunters is knowing what you want and having a good résumé to back it up. Headhunters tend to specialize. Read their ads carefully, then call and ask if they have positions available in your field. Most headhunters today accept résumés via fax and e-mail.

And last, but not least, let all your family and friends know you are looking for a new job. You would be amazed at what opportunities can develop. It helps if you're a good worker and a likable person.

Read Chapter 5 in *"Think and Grow Rich"* by Napoleon Hill. Then read it again.

PUTTING YOUR BEST FOOT FORWARD

A well-written résumé will get you in the door. After that, it's up to you. Depend on the résumé to open the door, not do the work for you. So what's the best way to write a résumé? From scratch. Go to your library and check out a book entitled *"The New Quick Job-Hunting Map"* (ISBN 0-89815-151-1) by Richard Nelson Bolles. This little $2.95 book contains an incredible skills-inventory list anyone can use as the foundation to write a successful résumé. Find the skills-inventory list on page 18 and begin writing down on a separate piece of paper all the skills, word for word, that relate to you. What you're looking for are words and phrases that best describe your skills. Write them down in no particular order. Just keep writing.

Once you're skills-inventory list is complete, move on to the next step. Have a separate piece of paper for each previous job position that will appear on your completed résumé. Now transfer each word or phrase to each previous job. When you're finished, most of the skills should be transferred to the job where you learned the skill.

Now the more demanding task is at hand. Take your skills for each position and make them flow into a concise paragraph that informs the reader of what you can do. This is easy and fun for me, although it might be the kiss of death to you. Give it a try! Or maybe you have a family member or friend who is gifted with words? If not, consider calling a nearby college journalism or English department. This effort may turn up talented students or an instructor who is willing to give you a helping hand for a nominal fee or nothing at all.

At this point, your résumé should be formatted in a page layout program like Quark Xpress or Aldus PageMaker. Try your library first. Most libraries have computers you can use. If not, Kinko's has a wonderful assortment of computer's that you can rent by the minute. Or enlist a friend, family member, or college student who has a computer to help you. It will be important to have a copy of your résumé on disk. For the more important positions you will need to slant your résumé toward that position.

A good résumé needs a good cover letter. Keep it short and to the point. Before you put that first-class stamp on the envelope, consider using Priority Mail for $3. It will attract attention. For more on building résumés and cover letters, ask your librarian for recommendations or visit your local bookstore. Ask what books on the subject are hot.

INCREASE YOUR VALUE
IN THE MARKETPLACE

If you desire higher wages you will need to increase your value in the marketplace. You get paid for the value you bring to the marketplace. You don't get paid for putting in time; you get paid for the value.

Is it possible to become twice as valuable to the marketplace and make twice as much money per hour? Yes. Three times as much? Yes. Ten times? Yes.

Why would someone make only $5 an hour? They're not very valuable to the marketplace. Valuable in the sight of God, yes. Valuable to others, yes. Valuable as a person, yes. But to the marketplace, that person is not very valuable. Where you start is not where you have to stay. It's a ladder, not a bed. You're expected to climb.

Why do some people earn $50 an hour? Evidently these people must be more valuable to the marketplace. Why do some people earn $500 an hour? Evidently they must be far more valuable to the marketplace.

Why would a company pay one person $1 million a year to run a company? If you helped a company make a billion dollars, $1 million is chicken feed.

You can go as far up this ladder as you want to. Here's how: *Work harder on yourself than you do on your job. If you work on your job you'll make a living; if you work on yourself you'll make a fortune.* There is plenty of room at the top of the ladder. It's the bottom that gets crowded.

THE SECRET OF THE WEALTHY

Have you ever wondered how wealthy people get wealthy? Have you ever asked yourself why poor people stay poor? Think about it. Wealthy people have 24 hours in each day. Poor people have the same 24 hours each day. *The secret of the wealthy is how they manage their time.* A better plan for how you will use your time will result in more money. Better plan—more money. Not, more money—better plan.

STEP THREE: HOW TO SPEND A DOLLAR

If you want your financial situation to change, *you* must change. One of the best lessons I ever received was from my friend Jim Rohn. Jim was broke at the age of 25, but within six years of applying the following principles he became a millionaire. When he was young, a millionaire friend of his asked him, "How much money have you saved in the last six years?" He answered, "None." His wise friend was astonished, and said, "Who sold you on that plan? You've bought into the wrong plan." Learn to invest first and spend what is left. If you continue to live the way you're living, the next six years will be exactly the same as the previous six. It's time you put someone else's philosophy to work for you.

So how does a wise person spend a dollar? The very first thing you do is give 10 percent of your earnings away each pay period. You decide whether you give from your gross or net income. If you want to be "grossly" blessed, give from your gross income. If you want to be "netly" blessed, give from your net income! Enlightened people know that giving starts the receiving process.

My wife and I chose to plant our first 10 percent into our home church. It's the first check she writes each week. If you don't have a home church, find a worthwhile charity.

The next 10 percent is set aside for what we call our active capital account. It's the fund established for saving for a down payment on a house, new car, secured bank card, secured bank loan, etc. Once we get beyond that, the money is saved until we have at least six months earnings. Wouldn't it be comforting to know if you lost your job today that you would have six months to find a new one?

The next 10 percent you pay to yourself. We call it our passive investment account. It's the account we never touch while it continues to accrue compound interest.

So there is it. We call this the 10-10-10 philosophy. It's the right way to spend a dollar. Consider the goal of living off 70 percent of your income. Less, if you have bigger dreams.

Some of you are staring into space right now. Okay, this is the ideal. We didn't start off by living on 70 percent of what we made. Giving 10 percent is mandatory for anyone desiring financial independence. Start to give today! The second 10 percent was a challenge, but it can be done. It took us over two years to reach that point. It's the third 10 percent that we just recently mastered. It took us a little over five years to reach the point of living off 70 percent of our income. Could we have done it sooner? Yes. We would encourage you to get started.

Begin to teach your kids these principles. The time to begin teaching them is now. A lot of the bad financial habits I grew up with I received from my parents. Children do what they see their parents doing. Our goal now is to live off 50 percent of our income within two years.

One way to start giving, saving and investing is to make these the first three checks you write. The amount you save and invest is not the important thing in the beginning; it's the habit you're trying to develop. The amounts will get larger as time goes on. Focus on developing the habit.

This was very difficult for me. I never saved any money when I was growing up. I would always spend it. Years later, my wife and I had to literally trick ourselves into starting our passive and active capital accounts. Here's what we did. Our banker gave us two secured loans, each with a monthly payment that equaled 10 percent of our monthly income. We now had a payment book and the chance of spoiling our perfect credit history if the payments were late. It worked. The monthly loan payments were made on time, and in two years not only did we get all that money we received back with interest, but we also re-established credit with a bank, and both loans appear on our credit reports.

This may seem drastic. But we were so caught up in making excuses for why we couldn't save or invest that we had to figure out a way to develop the habit. We knew that once we created the habit it would come easy. We discovered, things have a way of working out when they *must* work out.

BEATING THE CASH
POOR ARGUMENT

"...But, Stephen, there is no way we can give 10 percent of our income each pay period..." Then the next six years of your life will be just like the previous six years. "...But, Stephen, there is no way we can build up to paying ourselves 10 percent out of each paycheck each pay period..." Then the next six years of your life will be just like the previous six years. "...But, Stephen, there is no way we can invest 10 percent of our income each pay period..." Then the next six years of your life will be just like the previous six years. Get the idea? You cannot afford not to.

PROPER TIMING

Proper timing played an important role in each of our financial decisions. What about you? Any big cash bonuses coming up? Tax refund? Commission check? Birthday money? Christmas money? Can you sell anything you no longer need? Can you return things you bought within the last few months for credit?

With our first bank card, we needed $400, to begin the account. I verified with the company that they guaranteed to put a card in my hands in two weeks. With that in mind, we sacrificed $400 to begin the account, and the card arrived in exactly 14 days.

Sure, we had to eat spaghetti two weeks straight. But the sacrifice was worth it.

Our first car after bankruptcy was acquired with $500 cash and two post-dated checks for $1,300. We didn't have the $1,300, but we knew that if we didn't work hard to get it the car would be taken away. We came up with the money by saving everything we could and earning as much as we could. We did it.

Our second unsecured bank card is an excellent example of proper timing. With this bank the maximum credit limit on their card was $5,000. After 12 months of excellent payment history, the credit limit on your secured account automatically became your unsecured account limit. So the game was to raise the secured credit limit as high as possible. We decided to use the proceeds from our home equity loan to increase our secured credit limit before asking to be reviewed for unsecured status.

Our home equity loan closed the same month we were eligible to apply for unsecured status. We forwarded a cashier's check for $4,500 via FedEx to the bank. We gave them a few days to process the deposit, and called to verify that the account was paid off with a new secured credit limit of $5,000. We then placed a call to request being reviewed for unsecured status. In less than 10 days we had our $5,000 back and an unsecured bank card with a limit of $5,000 at 9.9%. Proper timing can mean everything. So play smart.

10

How to Interview
a Credit Lender

WHY EVEN BOTHER INTERVIEWING credit lenders? It seems like a
waste of time. Shouldn't *they* be interviewing *me*?

There are three main reasons to interview credit lenders. One is
to avoid unnecessary credit inquiries. The second is to determine
their credit guidelines before making an application. And third, to
evaluate all your options before you make a purchase decision.

As soon as we made the decision to file bankruptcy, I obtained
a copy of the Sunday newspaper from the largest city closest to
us. I wanted to talk with real estate agents and car dealers to see
what our options were.

It was comforting to know what my worst-case scenarios were
before I actually filed. You can use this method to determine what
your options are after bankruptcy as well. It's good to have plans
A, B, C and D. Chance favors a prepared mind.

Save yourself time and effort by always using the telephone to
interview lenders first. Take the time to visit the lender only when
you're sure they can help you.

CREDIT INQUIRIES

You have an enemy. It's called the "credit inquiry." Every time
you give someone permission to look at your credit report, it is
recorded for everyone to see for up to two years.

Credit lenders do not like credit inquiries. They get nervous
when they see too many of them. In fact, having too many credit
inquiries has been known to be the cause of denial for many
people applying for credit.

A credit inquiry that results in approved credit is okay. So is one that that occurs when you request a copy of your credit report from the credit bureau. It's the ones where you were declined credit that hurt you. This is the main reason you need to take a little more time and interview the credit lender. Avoid credit inquiries unless you are 99% convinced the lender will approve you. This can be difficult, especially when lenders cannot give you a definite answer until they review your credit file. Ask a lot of questions to several lenders, then go with your gut instinct.

One way around this obstacle is to ask the lender to review a recent credit file that you will provide. It's important to emphasize that you are trying to avoid unnecessary credit inquiries and that you will allow them to pull a credit file if you feel comfortable with their response from the credit file you provide. This works. I've done this with car dealers and mortgage companies. We used this method to purchase our first car and obtain our home equity loan.

Don't give out your Social Security number to anyone unless you're convinced they can help you. When you give out your SSN you give them permission to pull your credit reports.

BEFORE YOU CALL

Before you begin calling lenders there are a few things you must do. First, your call must go to the person handling the money. With that in mind, you must rehearse a 30-second "sound bite" of what you want. Read "*How to Get Your Point Across in 30 Seconds or Less*" by Milo Frank. A phone call to the new-car finance manager at a car dealership might go like this:

"Could I speak to the new-car lease financing manager, please? Thank you. Hello, Mr. Updike. My name is Stephen Snyder. I filed bankruptcy six months ago and am interested in leasing a car. Do you provide financing for people with a previous bankruptcy?..." Or:

"My name is Stephen Snyder. I filed bankruptcy six months ago and am interested in a car. I would prefer leasing a new car, but am open for your advice. I have re-established credit since the bankruptcy and have never been late since. The credit I have re-established is a Visa bank card and a bank loan. I have up to $500 I can put down, and can come up with more within 30 days. I have been employed for one year as a computer analyst and gross $2,000 a month. Can you help me?"

One of the questions they will ask you is why you filed bankruptcy. It's important how you answer this question. The best thing to say is the truth, but don't ramble unless they ask for more detail. Rehearse a 15-second "sound bite" as to the reason you filed bankruptcy. A good response might be:

> "We simply spent more money than we made. The bankruptcy was our wake-up call. And as you can tell by our timely payments, we've made a commitment to pay our bills early or on time."

The last thing a lender wants to hear is your "long story." Everyone likes to tell their story. But guess what? No one cares. All they want to know is whether your reason for filing bankruptcy will help them get what you need. Be short, concise, and to the point. 15 seconds is plenty of time.

The best reason for bankruptcy is: medical. This reason, if substantiated, will provide you more credibility. Just be sure you can support what you say. Remember, it's very easy to spot someone who isn't telling the truth. Your credit reports tells all.

CREDIT GUIDELINES

Ask what the lender's credit guidelines are. Why go through the process of filling out an application, waiting for an answer, risking a credit inquiry, with the probability of being turned down?

Some lenders will not tell you what their guidelines are. If they don't tell you, move on. It is not worth risking a credit inquiry.

I have found it beneficial to be very direct. "Do your credit guidelines permit extending credit to people with a previous bankruptcy?" Usually, if their response is "How long has it been since the bankruptcy?" I know I am talking with someone who knows what they are talking about.

Ninety-nine percent of the salespeople you talk to will not know what they are talking about. They are paid a certain minimum-wage per hour to follow a telephone script. Any deviation from the script will activate their "I better say something to sound intelligent" mode. Most of the time, what they say is wrong. It is best in this case to kindly ask to speak with a supervisor, the credit department, or someone who can answer specific questions concerning obtaining credit with that company.

Most of the time they will forward you to the "credit department." What you need to convey is that you are trying to avoid any unnecessary credit inquiries. You need to know what are the chances of getting an application approved with a previous bankruptcy. Back this statement up with affirming any new credit that you have re-established since the bankruptcy.

What you don't want to hear is this: "You must fill out an application, we will pull a credit report, and then be able to give you an answer." Be prepared; you will hear this a lot. I have a four-letter word for these people: N-E-X-T. If you are unable to convince the supervisor or credit department of your mission, move on to the next lender; this lender is not for you.

NEVER GIVE YOUR SOCIAL SECURITY NUMBER

By giving a lender your Social Security number, you give them permission to pull a credit report. Do not give out your Social Security number until you are convinced the lender can do what you ask. Let me repeat, do not give out your Social Security number until you are convinced the lender can do what you ask.

Too many people freely give out their Social Security number and end up with a lot of credit inquiries. Don't be fooled. When they ask for your SSN, say something like: "It's not necessary to give that to you yet. I don't want to risk a credit inquiry. When it's time, I will gladly give it to you. Next question?"

Some slick salespeople will say, "I will not pull a credit file until its necessary." Experience tells me not to believe them. Repeat your previous statement or blame it on a third party. One of my favorite lines in dealing with salespeople is: "My wife won't let me do that." It works.

Don't let someone push you into something you're not ready for yet. In addition, it's important to ask how many credit inquiries will appear on your credit file. Some car dealerships are particularly notorious for "shopping" your deal with several lenders. This may be okay if that dealership is the only one pulling your credit report and then faxes a copy to their lenders. It is not okay if each lender pulls a credit report on you to evaluate your application. Be sure.

I insist that they choose their best lender first. I tell them passionately about my quest to avoid unnecessary credit inquiries. If I am feisty that day, I usually say something like: "Shop my application to as many lenders who, if they turn me down, would agree to promptly remove the credit inquiry from my credit reports—otherwise I only want one credit inquiry."

TAKE NOTES

If you plan to interview several lenders, take good notes. After you talk with a few lenders you tend to forget exactly what each has told you. Take notes on things like: the person's name, title, lender's name, telephone, fax, hours of operation, work schedule, comments he/she made during your conversation, and any answers to your questions.

I also suggest that you grade each conversation. I use the "smiley face" method. If the conversation did not impress me I make a smiley face, but with a frown. If the conversation was neutral I made a straight line for his mouth. If the discussion was productive, insightful, and I felt I could trust the lender,

I made a smiley face with a big smile. Some even earned two smiley faces. In the end, those are the ones I usually did business with.

IN SUMMARY

1.   Prepare rehearsed "sound bites"

2.   Telephone each lender

3.   Ask about their credit guidelines

4.   Take notes

5.   Grade each conversation, using the "smiley face" method

6.   When appropriate, ask if they would review a recent credit report

7.   Make a decision which lender to start with

8.   Ask how many inquiries will show on your credit report

9.   Guard your Social Security number

10. Don't give up

11

The Art of Filling Out a Credit Application

THE FIRST STEP TO filling out any credit application begins with assembling all your information in one place. I call it the "new credit" folder. It's as simple as using a manila folder, labeling it, and storing it in a safe place.

Your "new credit folder" will contain several items:

- Copies of your discharge letter
- A one-page letter of explanation as to why you filed bankruptcy (preferably edited by one of your lenders)
- A copy of your recent credit report from all three major credit reporting agencies
- Copies of previous credit applications
- Facts about you and your spouse
- Summary page of new credit since the bankruptcy
- Copy of complete bankruptcy paperwork

All lenders will request a copy of your discharge letter. Have several copies available. Only a few lenders, usually mortgage-related, will request a complete copy of your bankruptcy paperwork.

A one-page letter of explanation as to why you filed bankruptcy will be necessary for anything mortgage-related. This is a great time to fine-tune your story so someone can quickly understand your situation. Take some time to create a good letter. It's always a good idea to ask the lender exactly what the letter should say. Attitude is really important here. They may even write it for you. Or at the least, make corrections to your letter before sending it off to the underwriter.

Ask which credit reporting agency the lender uses. Be sure to have a recent copy of this credit report. Each of your three credit reports are different. Some lenders report to all three major credit reporting agencies, others do not. In Indianapolis, Equifax and Trans Union are the most common credit reporting agencies. Experian may be your primary credit reporting agency. All mortgage lenders subscribe to a mortgage reporting service that combines all three reports into one. Other lenders just use the primary reporting agency in your area.

It's always a good idea to copy your signed credit application before turning it into the lender. Not only does it help you keep track of what you said, but you can refer back to it if necessary. Consistency is important.

It seems I can never remember my parents' address, my nearest relatives' telephone number, my wife's Social Security number, our previous addresses, bank account numbers, wife's birthday, employer's address and telephone, date started employment, driver's license numbers, or other types of information on a credit application. Put all this information in one place; it will save you time and make your credit applications consistent.

The most important information in your "new credit" folder is the summary of your new credit since the bankruptcy. This will become an important sales tool. At first there won't be much on it, but over time it will grow.

I suggest keeping track of a few things: name of credit lender, address, telephone number, account number, type of account (joint or individual), date opened, balance, monthly payment, and high credit limit.

It is important to be accurate. If you come across as being accurate to the penny, lenders will assume you're accurate in everything else as well. People who exaggerate in one area usually exaggerate in many areas. So be accurate. You need every advantage you can get early on.

FILL OUT AND REPLY TO EVERY QUESTION

It seems simple. But a lot of people ignore this. Remember, you need as much in your favor as you can get. Failure to answer questions may become a red flag in the underwriter's eyes.

TELL THE TRUTH

Be honest when you fill out the credit application. It's the best policy. However, always round numbers upward in your favor. For instance, if the question is "How long have you lived at your present address?" and you have lived there one year and 11 months, it's okay to round upward and just write two years. This is a judgment call on your part, but it is my experience that this is acceptable.

WRITE LEGIBLY

It's important that whoever fills out the credit application can communicate clearly. An application that is hard to read is a red flag. It could mean you're hiding something or that you have a very low education level. Find someone who can fill it out legibly.

SKIP OVER THE "HAVE YOU EVER FILED BANKRUPTCY?" QUESTION

I personally had a problem with this one. To me it seemed to be dishonest. The best thing to do is ask the salesperson taking your application if you should ignore that question or not. Some companies automatically reject applications when that box is checked, and it is difficult for the salesperson to work in your favor after the fact. It is much easier to ignore the question and allow the salesperson to work on your behalf with the underwriter.

Some car dealerships take your written application, then input your data into a computer. The most knowledgeable salespeople automatically ignore this question for you, even though you may have checked "yes" on the application. If you have reservations, clearly communicate to your salesperson your situation and ignore the question.

UNDERSTANDING POINT SCORING SYSTEMS

Many lending institutions use a point scoring system to determine the eligibility of a borrower. In this system, a numeric value is assigned to different categories. This numeric value measures the different variables as to a person's stability, income, credit history, expenses, etc.

The number of points required for eligibility for a loan will vary from bank to bank, but even within the same bank, the criteria will change depending on the nation's current economic conditions. When the money supply is plentiful, the banks will lower their criteria. When the money market is "tight," the banks will tighten their requirements. The following is an example of a point scoring system:

Category	*Points*
Employment	
1 year or less at present employment	0
1-2 years	1
2-4 years	2
4-10 years	3
Over 10 years	4
Monthly income (gross)	
Less than $1,000	0
$1,000 to $1,500	1
$1,500 to $2,000	2
Over $2,000	3
Length at present address	
Less than 3 years	0
3 years or more	1
Savings account	
No	0
Yes	1
Checking account	
No	0
Yes, but with 5 returned items this year	1
Yes, but with no returned items this year	2

Previous loan with this bank

No	0
Yes, but still open	0
Yes, but closed with 2 or less late pays	1

Credit references

No	0
Yes	1

Obligations past due

Yes	0
No	1

Monthly obligations vs. income

50%	0
40% to 49%	1
30% to 39%	2
Less than 30%	3

Own real estate

No	0
Yes	3

Telephone listed in applicant's name

No	0
Yes	1

Age of automobile

Over 1 year	0
Less than 1 year	1

Summary

90% - 100% of possible points
        Loans guaranteed automatically
70% - 90% of possible points
        Loans guaranteed unless there
        is a good reason to deny
50% - 70% of possible points
        Reasonable risk; review toward approval
40% - 50% of possible points
        Review application toward rejection
0% - 40% of possible points
        Reject application

UNDERSTANDING YOUR DEBT-TO-INCOME RATIO

The most common method to determine how financially fit you are is to figure out your debt-to-income ratio.

A debt-to-income ratio is the most widely used method for determining if a consumer has too much debt in relation to income. This ratio can be figured on a monthly or annual basis. A monthly debt-to-income ratio provides a good indication of how strong your financial situation is on a day-to-day basis.

The best way to understand is to actually do it. Begin by gathering your most recent credit billing statements. Don't include your mortgage or rent, utilities or taxes as debts here.

It is very important to work with accurate numbers. If you do not have a current billing statement, call the creditor and ask for your current payment due and the balance on your account.

List all your bills in one column. In a second column, list your monthly payments. In a third column, list the current outstanding balance you still owe on these bills.

Next, determine your monthly income. Start with your annual gross income (income before taxes). Add any additional income you receive. Do not include additional income that is not guaranteed. If you earn an hourly wage instead of a salary, take an average weekly paycheck and multiply that figure by 52 (weeks) to determine your gross annual income. You can then divide that figure by 12 to determine your monthly income.

Divide your monthly payments by your total monthly income. The answer is your monthly debt-to-income ratio. The number you end up with will be a percentage, so if you're doing it manually, move the decimal point two spaces to the right.

MONTHLY BILLS

Lender	Payment	Balance
Toyota	320.00	10,240
Mazda	299.97	7,199
Bank One Visa	110.00	4,500
Orchard Bank	45.00	1,400
First Indiana Bank	152.00	14,000
Totals	926.97	37,339

MONTHLY INCOME

Annual gross income (Michele)	36,400
Bonuses (Michele)	7,200
Annual gross income (Stephen)	12,000
Bonuses (Stephen)	12,000
Total annual income	67,600
Total monthly income	5,633

MONTHLY DEBT-TO-INCOME RATIO

Monthly debt payments	926.97
Monthly income	5,633
Debt-to-income ratio	16.37%

WHAT DOES IT MEAN?

If your debt-to-income ratio is:
  15 percent or less: You are probably in good shape.
  15 to 20 percent: Most financial advisors consider a 20
    percent ratio a safe level. Others consider it somewhat high.
  20 to 35 percent: You should probably cut back.
  35 to 50 percent: You have too much debt.
  50 percent or more: Make an appointment with a financial
    advisor. If not, you may be headed for bankruptcy again.

RED FLAGS ON A CREDIT APPLICATION

There are certain things you want to avoid. These serve as "red flags" to lenders who review your application:

Bankruptcy
High debt-to-income ratio
Foreigners without permanent resident status
Post office box as mailing address
Frequent changes in employment (unrelated occupations)
Self-employed
No telephone number
Telephone not listed in applicant's name
Unskilled laborers
Glamour jobs that pay poorly
Excessive numbers of revolving charge cards for applicants
   with modest income
Employers with unverifiable telephone number
No checking or savings account

HELP FOR ENTREPRENEURS

One out of five people who file for bankruptcy protection are entrepreneurs. Credit can be difficult to obtain if you are self-employed. Self-employed people are generally viewed as being high credit risks. Being an employee of your own corporation is not viewed as being self-employed.

The challenge to entrepreneurs is to make yourself appear as "normal" and "stable" as the rest of the bill-paying public. It might be helpful to know that all of our credit was obtained when both my wife and I were self-employed. A few things we recommend:

1.   Get incorporated! There are a lot of good books on the
      subject at your library. Consider filing your own
      paperwork with the Secretary of State.

2.   Do not name your corporation after yourself. A
      corporation carrying your own name is a dead giveaway

that it's your own company.

3.   Hire yourself as an employee of the corporation and pay yourself a salary. The minute a lender feels that you are self-employed, they ask for tax returns and several years of paperwork, and maybe even profit-and-loss statements. Why go through the trouble?

4.   If you work out of your home, rent a commercial postal box with a familiar address for your business street address. Instead of using Box 0000, be sure the address is a street address, and you can have a suite number at the end.

5.   Create an interactive voice response (IVR) system for your company. Ours was professionally created, and when called by lenders it was very convincing. In fact, no one has ever called to verify employment of income. Today there is a device that does the same thing for under $300. Call 1-888-TINA-789 or access their web site at: *http://www.dcint.com/products.html.*

For more detailed information on how to overcome the self-employed issue, contact After Bankruptcy Foundation at 1-317-578-7118. Ask for the "audiotape for self-employed." There's a small fee for the tape, but it is the best information on the subject.

WHAT TO DO IF YOU'RE TURNED DOWN

IF YOU DO YOUR homework and follow what we outline in this book you will rarely, if ever, hear the word "no" after you turn in a credit application.

However, if you do experience a "no" the best thing to do is immediately turn it into a free credit report.

All the major credit reporting agencies will give you a free copy of your credit report if you have been turned down for credit within 60 days. Take advantage of it.

If you're like me and refuse to take "no" for an answer, the next step is to go higher. Ask to speak with a supervisor.

My friend Steve applied for an unsecured bank card through a special program offered by a local bank. He was turned down. He quickly called back and asked a supervisor to reconsider the decision. Within 10 days he had his bank card.

Sometimes lenders pigeon hole people with a previous bankruptcy. The first "no" doesn't always mean "no." It's just how their system works.

If you call back and they still will not approve you, ask questions. Try to learn as much from the experience to benefit you in the days, weeks, and months to come. Ask the person what they feel would increase your chances of obtaining credit the next time around. Ask what they would do if they were you. Ask for a referral of someone who may be able to help you. Thank them for their time, and move on.

12

Personal Development 101

The following few pages are a summary of the audiobook "Success! The Glenn Bland Method." It is, in my opinion, the best book available on personal development, and applies so closely to my message that I decided to purchase the rights to the audiobook version and reprint it here. It's my gift to you. The book is available by special order through your local bookstore. Enjoy.

IF I DREW A line and told you that simply stepping over it would guarantee inner peace, riches, enlightenment and physical well-being, would you take that step? Stepping across the line does work. I've seen derelicts changed into decent people. Debt-ridden individuals into financial successes. Misguided souls into persons who possess the wisdom of the ages. Mentally and physically ill weaklings into healthy and productive citizens.

Years of thought, study and planning preceded the development of the Bland Method of goal setting and planning. The heart of these teachings can direct you to a life of happiness and success. The principles in my method are not unique. They've been responsible for the making of kings, the building of empires and the creation of vast fortunes.

My method of goal setting and planning had its beginning many years ago when I first became success-conscious. At that time in my life I was doing my work well. But only because it was something I had to do. I was drifting, I had no direction, no goals, no plans. I didn't understand the one basic principle. Men who have goals and plans dictate to others, while men who have no goals or plans are dictated to. I read this principle in a book called *"Think and Grow Rich"* by Napoleon Hill. As I read I said to myself, "He has found the key that can unlock the door to happiness and success in my life. This is what I've been looking for."

Success consciousness is the place where all achievement begins. It's when you first realize that there is a happy and successful way to live. You suddenly know you can change your life for the better. I read many books, spent many hours listening to records and tapes with only one goal: to program my mind for happiness and success. As I studied, I hit upon a basic truth. Techniques and methods change, but principles never do. I knew at that moment where to find the information I had been searching for. Everything you and I need to know about happiness and success is contained within the Bible. The Bible contains the answers to all of life's opportunities and problems. From the wellspring of the Creator stimulating wisdom will never run dry. We are limited in our understanding only by our willingness to abide by the principles and to grow.

Mankind faces great problems today because people have become so self-sufficient that they sometimes forget there is a God. We forget that there is an omnipresent power bigger and more powerful than you or me. God created everything that exists, and He certainly can create happiness and success for a man if that man will play the game according to the rules. The Bible is no mere book, for through its message the secret of happiness and success will become a reality in your life. You'll be asked to do only one thing as these principles are unfolded for you: believe.

History reveals that there have always been those individuals who spend their lives in a negative world where "can't" is the most frequently used word in their vocabulary. But one of the most important and basic natural laws of the universe is: Anything you can think of and believe in, you can achieve. Jesus made the same point. If you can believe, all things are possible to him that believes. Jesus didn't eliminate anything; He said, "all things." Belief is a powerful force, and when properly used it can move man to accomplish great things. Our Creator gave us the choice of living in two worlds, positive or negative. A world where you can accomplish your lifetime dreams or a world where you can't do anything because a million trivial excuses hold you back. Decide that you are going to be a member of that select group of successful people who live in a positive world. Take the "can't" out of your life by believing. Mankind has always been aware of God's creative force.

The evidence of this great force is found in the birth of an infant, in the roar of an ocean wave, in the unparalleled beauty of a flower and in the magnificent design of a single snowflake. Each of us has the opportunity to use this creative force to accomplish our goals, but few do so. This creative force has been given to us free. To receive its full power we must only believe. The statement "The best things in life are free" is true. They are the things that are responsible for putting happiness in your life.

To take advantage of the natural laws of the universe, we must understand the essence of the Creator who governs all life and creation.

Sovereign:	The Creator is the ruler of all things.
Righteous:	It is impossible for the Creator to be wrong.
	He is perfect in every way.
Just:	The Creator knows everything.
	Therefore, it's impossible for Him to be unfair.
Eternal:	The Creator has always existed;
	He is everlasting.
Omnipotent:	The Creator knows everything.
Omnipresent:	The Creator is everywhere at all times.
Immutable:	The Creator never changes.
	He is the same yesterday, today and forever.
Truthful:	The Creator is absolutely true.
	It is impossible for Him to lie.

The Creator established the rules, and simply playing the game with all of your heart will produce fantastic rewards. Before going on, take these two steps:

Convince yourself that there is a happier and more successful way of living than your present way of life; and

Accept the fact that God is a tremendous guiding force in this universe and that He is wiser and more powerful than you.

How would you define success? There are probably as many different definitions as there are people in the world. A businessman might say that being successful means earning a lot of money. A football coach may believe that the pinnacle of success is winning the national championship. To a salesman, success means becoming the number one producer with his company. To the architect, success would probably be beautiful creations on his city's skyline.

Everyone may have a personal definition for success, but success is more than any of the preceding definitions. True success avoids extremes. It's a gradual process. Through balanced living you'll find happiness and success. Our Creator intends for you and me to lead happy and successful lives by applying the natural laws established by Him to keep us in tune with the universe. If I were to choose one word to define our Creator, it would be balance.

Consider the perfect balance between the plant and animal worlds, each complementing the other, so that both will survive. Our Creator provided for everything. He is aware of all of our opportunities, as well as all of our problems. Great people lead balanced lives, which are made meaningful by belief. William B. Walton, president of Holiday Inn, spoke of his four great loves. They were: love of God, love of family, love of country and love of work. His idea of success was woven with the threads of direction, balance and belief. Coach Vince Lombardi guided his players with the following statement: "There are only three things that are important in your life: your God, your family and the Green Bay Packers." Again, you should see the threads of direction, balance and belief woven throughout this statement. Any definition of success must contain these threads of truth.

Direction is setting your sights on things that are worthwhile and then establishing a plan to work toward their fulfillment and accomplishment. Balance is keeping the proper perspective about every area of your life. Staying in harmony with nature's laws produces a perfect balance. Balance in all things brings about happiness, and no man will become successful who does not possess belief. The greater his belief, the greater his degree of success. With these three ingredients as a foundation, we can define success. *"Success is the progressive realization of predetermined worthwhile goals stabilized with balance and purified by belief."*

Here are seven dynamic rules to help you put this definition to work immediately:

1. Let God guide you. Get yourself out of the way and let the great creative mind of God give you direction. Have faith.

2. Establish a faith period. Set aside 30 minutes each morning to engage in meditation and planning.

3. Crystallize your goals. Decide on specific goals you want to achieve, and keep them before you each day.

4. Make a plan of action. Develop a blueprint for achieving your goals and a target date for their accomplishment.

5. Develop a burning desire. Desire for the things you want in life will motivate you to action.

6. Believe in yourself. You can accomplish anything if you believe you can.

7. Never give up. Success cannot elude a will that stays in existence in spite of the pressures of adversity. Success comes to persistent people. It may require changing your entire way of life to apply the dynamic success plan, but remember, successful men do things that failures never get around to doing.

Carefully protected by your cranium, you carry with you the most intricate and baffling computer ever conceived—your mind. This fantastic computer of yours was created by God's infinite intelligence. It's capable of conceiving any idea you'll ever need. Despite its wealth-giving potential, the mind is used by most people at about 10% of its potential. We occupy our minds with insignificant things, instead of letting them soar to accomplish big and important things. Your mind is the computer and you are the computer programmer. If you put positive information in, the results will be positive and worthwhile. If you feed your mind negative information, the results will be directed toward failure. In the Bible we find, "As a man thinks in his heart, so is he." You're guided by your mind, and you must live upon the fruits of your thoughts. Since we become what we think about, then it's most important that we carefully regard our thought patterns. Developing right thinking is not easy, because it involves establishing new habits, which take days, weeks, months, often years before they become an integral part of your life.

New habits are not easily formed, especially when they must replace entrenched bad habits—but it can be done. If you strive to be happy and successful, establish good habits, because while in the beginning you make your habits, in the end your habits make you.

Each of us has bad habits and negative thoughts that hold us back and keep us from becoming the dynamic person that lives within. Now is the time to put away the cloak of failure, worn in the negative life, and replace it with a shiny new suit of armor, called success doctrine. How can you get your suit of armor? Well, the first step to acquiring success doctrine is deciding that you want to become happy, successful, and to possess great wisdom. You may need to reprogram your thinking so that you can truly hold the key to happiness in your hand. You'll not gain this wisdom overnight. Your negative thoughts will not suddenly disappear. It takes time to replace negativism with positiveness. It's a gradual process.

Now that we've established that thoughts have power, that thoughts become reality, and that by programming your mind with positive thoughts you can become a positive person let me explain how to build a success complex in your life. A success complex has six steps, which are backwards:

6. Mastery of the details of life
5. Capacity to love
4. Relaxed mental attitude

3.   Inner happiness
2.   Success orientation
1.   Success doctrine or wisdom

Step 1. Imagine for a moment that you are a master builder and that you've been hired to construct a six-story building. You select the strongest supports and the best materials in designing the foundation. Without a firm foundation the structure cannot stand. It would crumble and fall. The full weight of the other five stories will rest upon this firm foundation. Success doctrine is a firm foundation on which your future can be built. The Bible says, *"Wisdom gives a long good life, riches, honor, pleasure and peace."* (Proverbs 3:16-17) *"He who loves wisdom loves his own best interest and will be a success."* That's Proverbs 19:8. You gain wisdom by becoming a student. You read, you study, you listen, and you must do these things each day on a planned and organized basis. It must become part of your life. You must eat, sleep and drink success doctrine. *"I, Wisdom, will make the hours of your day more profitable and the years of your life more fruitful."* That's Proverbs 9:11.

Step 2. You'll be success-oriented when you understand yourself, and you can then begin to understand others. The world will truly be your oyster, for you will be a wise person. One who possesses the wisdom of the ages, a man who believes.

Step 3. Everyone in the world seems to be searching for inner happiness. You find inner happiness as soon as you possess success doctrine and become success-oriented. Because you understand the Creator and His natural laws, your life will be in complete harmony with the world around you. This generates inner peace and happiness.

Step 4. Once you have success doctrine in the front of your mind and it becomes success-oriented and possesses inner happiness, you will develop a relaxed mental attitude. You'll then have everything under control. The Bible says *a relaxed attitude lengthens a man's life.* That's Proverbs 14:30. Belief fosters a relaxed mind.

Step 5. The next important step in the success complex is acquiring the capacity to love. Don't confuse this with the selfish humanistic love found so often in society today. This is the true, complete and unselfish love the apostle Paul talked about in I Corinthians. *If I gave everything I had to poor people and were burned alive for preaching the Gospel, but did not love others, it would be of no value whatsoever.* Even as great a man as the Apostle Paul readily admitted that without the capacity to love, everything else is meaningless. With success doctrine you will have a deeper and more meaningful feeling for your family and your fellow men.

Step 6. The pinnacle of the success doctrine is the mastery of the details of life. Most people find it difficult to meet the daily trials and tribulations, but those who possess success doctrine know how to organize themselves through goals, plans and priorities to handle anything that comes up. The individual with success doctrine learns to solve what he can and to live with what he can't without destroying his peace of mind.

Most people want to be success-oriented, have inner happiness, display a relaxed mental attitude, possess the capacity to love, and want to be able to master the details of life. Few are willing to pay the price, however, of gaining the success doctrine.

Imagine that you are an internationally known architect commissioned to supervise the construction of the world's tallest and most beautiful building. The materials are piled high. The contractors are surrounded by their workmen. You give the command "Build me a building." The first question on the lips of every craftsman and contractor would be, Where's the blueprint? A master craftsman must have a plan. He can't effectively use his talents unless he has guidelines to direct his genius. You are the architect of your own life. You can construct happiness and success, or a life filled with misery and failure. The blueprint is the key. People with goals and plans succeed in life, while people without them fail. We are living at a point in world history when people wander restlessly about looking for something that can't be explained. They're confused, frustrated and filled with anxiety, and they can't understand why. There's only one solution. Man must go back to the basic fundamentals of skillful living given to him by the Creator, the great natural laws of the universe. Ecclesiastes 7:13 reads, *"See the way the Creator does things and fall into line. Don't fight the facts of nature. You can't beat Him, so you might as well join Him and let His natural laws work for you and not against you."*

One of the best-known natural laws of the universe is the law of gravity. If you climb to the top of a tall building and jump off, you'll fall down. You never fall up. You can't see, smell or touch the law of gravity, but you know it's there. So it is with the natural laws of happiness and success. You can't see, smell, or touch them, but they are there. Operate within the framework of these laws, and happiness and success will be yours for the taking. The holy Bible is the Creator's plan for the ages. Goals and plans are the magic keys to happiness and success. Goals and plans made within the framework of natural law take the worry out of living. Conformity to God's laws frees your mind so that you may get on with your opportunities.

There are four reasons most people don't set goals and establish plans. They are:

(1)   They don't know why
(2)   It's too much trouble
(3)   They don't have faith in their goals and plans after they're developed
(4)   They begin on a long-range basis, and this prevents them from seeing immediate results, so they become discouraged

If one of these reasons is holding you back, the Bland method of goal setting and planning will solve your problem.

My method teaches the principles of short-range and long-range planning, enabling you to discover immediately that planning really works. My method is based on natural law, which will give you the confidence and faith you need to stick with the program. Take time to establish definite goals and plans for yourself. You will find that the most difficult part of the process is carrying out your plans once they've been committed to writing. You'll encounter temporary defeats many times, but by sticking with the program you'll charge through adverse situations like an all-pro running back on his way to the goal line. Remember, out of every adversity comes an equal or greater opportunity.

In Houston, Texas, several years ago a great sports arena was planned, the first of its kind. A glass roof would cover the arena so that sporting events could be conducted under perfect climactic conditions despite Mother Nature. But when the magnificent structure was completed, grass wouldn't grow on the playing field. The developers had a multi-million-dollar sports complex that had become worthless. This adversity resulted in the discovery of an artificial playing surface, even better than grass. Today, artificial turf covers many outdoor stadiums across the nation. Out of adversity comes opportunity. Welcome adversity; it's your springboard to great achievement.

As you begin to formulate goals in your mind, dare to think big. For example, let's say that my income for the past year was $15,000. I set a goal for the coming year of $35,000. After working hard to attain my new objective I found that I had earned only $28,483. Did I fail? Certainly not. I didn't gain my goal of $35,000 in income, but look at the fantastic progress that was made. Dare to aim high, as long as you sincerely believe that you can reach your goal at some time in the future.

It's wise to use the counsel of other qualified people when you set goals and make plans. Proverbs 15:22 says, *"Plans go wrong with too few counselors; many counselors bring success."* I suggest that you choose one or two individuals whose judgment and ability you greatly respect, and form a success council for the purpose of exchanging ideas regarding each individual's goals and plans. The Bible says, *"The intelligent man is always open to new ideas. In fact, he looks for them."* That's Proverbs 18:15. And in Ecclesiastes *"Two can accomplish more than twice as much as one. For the results can be much better. If one falls, the other pulls him up. Three is even better, for a triple-braided cord is not easily broken."* (Ecclesiastes 4:9 and 12) *"Be with wise men and become wise."* (Proverbs 13:20)

For your success council to function properly, there must be complete harmony among the members. There can be no negativism, or the group will destroy each individual involved. Stay away from negative people, because they'll program you for failure. Guide group thinking by establishing positive guidelines, and schedule regular meetings with time for each member to make a personal progress report. This provides the follow-through necessary for individual goals and plans to become reality. Just setting a goal and making your plans to attain it are not enough. You must also set a date when you wish to attain the goal. It could be as short as an hour, or it could be five years or 65 years.

In 1960 President John F. Kennedy addressed the nation, announcing the beginning of a 10-year space program designed to put a man on the moon. Let's analyze why this effort was such a huge success.

> First, a definite goal was selected. A man on the moon.
> Second, there was a basic plan.
> Third, there was a target date, 10 years.

There was a fourth procedure employed on this project. After the first three steps—a goal, a plan and a target date—it was necessary to constantly keep the goal before them each day. There were many unknowns, but the men and women engaged in the moon shot project kept their goal constantly before them. They used group thinking and maintained their faith through temporary defeat. Because they believed their goal would be accomplished, the United States successfully landed a man on the moon with one year to spare.

Let me repeat the steps the space project took.

> First, a goal was set.
> Second, a plan was made.
> Third, a firm target date was established.
> Fourth, group thinking was employed.
> Fifth, everyone kept the goal constantly in mind.

Sixth, action was applied.
And seventh, they fervently kept the faith.
It was impossible for them to fail.

Now, we reach the most important phase of the goal-setting and planning process. The principles already presented will bring material success into your life, but they will not bring happiness. True happiness can only be achieved by living a balanced life. Balance is the key for us. All the natural laws brought into being by the Creator are based on the natural law of balance. Each of us needs to learn to live within the boundaries of this great natural law. If you're in balance with the world around you, you'll be happy. If you're out of balance with the world around you, you'll be unhappy. Your life is made up of four major areas: spiritual, financial, educational and recreational. Without proper blend and emphasis upon these four areas, your life will be out of balance, and you'll be unhappy.

AREA ONE—spiritual balance. Do you know someone who's spiritually out of balance? Perhaps you know someone who is so obsessed with things of the spiritual nature that he's a fanatic and people avoid him. He's overbalanced in one area. Or perhaps you know someone who has no spiritual life at all. These examples are two extremes, but each illustrates spiritual imbalance. Man's very nature embodies an innate drive to worship something, and the Bible says *there should be only one object of worship, the Creator.* Make definite spiritual plans for you and your family to enjoy the balanced fullness and meaningfulness of life. You'll never be sorry.

AREA TWO—financial balance. Perhaps you have a friend who is financially out of balance. This individual is driven by money alone. The pursuit of it has caused a complete collapse of his personal life and family harmony. In Ecclesiastes 5:10 we find, *"He who loves money shall never have enough. The foolishness of thinking that wealth brings happiness."* At the opposite extreme, an individual to whom money means nothing fails to provide for his own and lives in poverty. This individual has just as serious a financial imbalance as the person who is money-mad. Somewhere between these two extremes is a place of perfect balance. In almost every case the single biggest problem people face is the handling of money. Most people simply don't understand that they can't have both money and things. At least in the beginning. To accumulate money you must give up things. But if you accumulate things, you will never have money. If you sincerely want to accumulate money there are seven things you must do.

1. Don't charge. Charge accounts and credit cards get people into financial trouble. Remember what Proverbs 22:7 says, *"Just as the rich rule the poor, so the borrower is the servant to the lender."*

2. Don't consolidate your bills. This is popular, but it doesn't always work. You may consolidate bills into one monthly payment at extreme high interest rates and end up with the consolidated debt to pay, plus many new ones if the old, bad money-management habits haven't been changed.

3. Don't buy impulsively. When you desire to purchase anything of consequence, write it down. Wait one month, then, if you still want it, consider working it into your budget. You'll often discover that your desire was only a passing fancy.

4. Establish a budget. Keep records of your income and expenses. Decide exactly what you will spend for necessities and luxuries each month and then stick with it. Watch every penny.

5. Pay yourself first. Every time you receive your paycheck, put something aside for yourself. At first the amount may be small, but this will grow because you are forming a good habit. A habit of saving. Proverbs 21:20 says, *"The wise man saves for the future, but the foolish*

man spends whatever he gets."

6.   How to pay monthly bills. When you write checks each month, write them in this order: church or some worth while charity, savings, insurance for security, food, shelter, and then finally all other things. This procedure will help you provide for the necessary things first and let other things take care of themselves.

7.   Investing. There are five steps to good money management. Putting these five steps to work will provide financial security in your life.

   a.   Basic needs. You must provide food, clothing and shelter before investing in other things. For those who progress beyond providing these basic needs for their families, the next step is...

   b.   Insurance. Protect yourself from possible financial disasters with life, health and casualty insurance. For those who manage to provide basic needs and insurance, the next step is...

   c.   Cash fund. Build a cash fund for emergencies and opportunities that come along. Build a savings account until it equals six months of your income. For those who build this cash fund, the next step is...

   d.   Unimproved land. Investing in unimproved land is a relatively safe investment with a very high return. The value of land should never decrease, so at this point in your accumulation of wealth, buy unimproved land. Some people can provide for basic needs, insurance, cash fund, and unimproved land and never proceed farther. For those who do, the next step is...

e.   Stocks and bonds. This is properly the last step
         because it's speculative investment. This step
         can prove to be risky, and caution should always
         be exercised when engaging in this type of
         investment.

These are the five steps to good money management. Normally,
the only problem arises if you decide that the five steps are too
slow. You decide that you want to make it quick and jump all the
way to step five. When you do so, look out. You're headed for
financial disaster. Stick with the five steps. They work.

Remember, the Bible does not say that money is evil. The Bible
does say *the "love of money is the root of all evil."* That's 1
Timothy 6:10. When you begin to accumulate money in large
amounts, many good and evil opportunities, never available to
you before, will tempt you. Jesus said, *"It's easier for a camel to
go through the eye of a needle than for a rich man to enter the
Kingdom of Heaven."* The temptation to do evil is great when
you have an abundance of money, and if you become a slave to
money it will destroy your peace of mind and your relationship
with the Creator, but this need not happen if you have firmly
entrenched sound goals and plans to guide you. Many rich men
have entered into the Kingdom of perfect peace and harmony that
the Creator planned for them. It can be done through goals and
plans that keep the pathway to happiness and success open.

The way in which you regard money is extremely important.
When you love money, you have financial imbalance. Money has
become the master, rather than the slave. No one can attain riches
unless they enrich others. The Bible tells us that *God loves a
cheerful giver and will return his gifts many times over if the gifts
are given with the right attitude.* You can't give with the
expectation of getting. When gifts are given unselfishly, with
nothing expected in return, they'll be returned many times over.

Just where are you going to get the money so that you can start
giving some away? Well, there's only one source: the money you
earn. That must come from some beneficial service you can
render to your fellow man. Do you need to find some service to
render? Probably not; most people can render a beneficial service

in their present work. You probably have a virtual gold mine right where you are. Don't overlook the obvious. Establish your goals and make your plans to render the best possible service in your present work. Money will come to you on a sound basis in only one way. The formula: service, success, then money.

There is a price to be paid for success. In addition to the long years of preparation, there must be dedication to service. The price is no different, no matter what your occupation may be. If you sincerely want to earn money, you must be prepared to pay the price: service.

We have already discussed the importance of the first two areas for true happiness—spiritual and financial. To attain true balance, two additional areas are essential.

Area three is educational, and if this is not in harmony with the other principles, your journey toward happiness will be erratic, if not impossible. The fourth area, recreational, meets the needs expressed in the old saying, "All work and no play makes Jack a dull boy." Without relaxation and satisfactory balance, Jack is headed for a breakdown.

AREA THREE—educational balance. Have you ever known an individual who was educationally out of balance? He has become so obsessed with gaining knowledge that he becomes an educated fool. He's so technical in his thinking that the forgets how to apply his knowledge in practical situations. He never seems to find a way to use knowledge to benefit himself and his family. Then there is the individual who possesses little or no education. He and his family must suffer the consequences of insufficient education throughout their lives. Both extremes illustrate educational imbalance. Somewhere between these two extremes is a place of perfect educational balance. You arrive at this point through goal-setting and planning in the educational area.

There are two kinds of knowledge: general and specialized. Generalized knowledge can help you become a more well-rounded person, but it doesn't necessarily help you earn your living. The knowledge that will guide you in your work and form the foundation for setting goals and establishing plans is called specialized knowledge. Specialized knowledge is knowing your business through experience and study. Engage in at least one organized educational activity a year. This educational experience will prevent your mind from becoming stagnant and unproductive and will keep you mentally alert so that you may perform at peak efficiency. You can do this in several different ways: through formal classroom programs, correspondence courses or individual study. Do it on a planned basis and for the purpose of gaining specialized knowledge. If you are a person of normal intelligence and have the willingness to work and the desire to obtain specialized knowledge, you can succeed.

AREA FOUR—recreational balance. Have you ever known someone with a recreational imbalance? There are two types. The first recreates himself right into financial disaster. He wants to play all the time, never giving enough attention to the spiritual, financial and educational areas of his life. The man with the second type of recreational imbalance enjoys no recreational pleasures at all. He keeps his nose to the grindstone, never having enough time for such, as he calls them, foolish things as physical exercise and relaxation. These two extreme cases point up the need for balance. Planned recreation is important to our physical and mental well-being. A strong body and a sound mind must function in harmony for success. The Bible says, *"That any enterprise is built by wise planning. Becomes strong through common sense and profits wonderfully by keeping abreast of the facts."* That's Proverbs 24:3 and 4.

Definite goals and plans are important to you as an individual, but they are equally important to your entire family. Setting family goals and establishing definite plans for their fulfillment is a tremendous positive force. Choose a worthwhile goal and then release yourself from your old self and go to that goal. No one can stop a man with a plan.

We live in a very complex world. Our modern environment does not automatically create a wholesome atmosphere for slowing down. Consequently, we miss the miraculous blessings that are ours for the taking. Get the most out of your life by setting aside 30 minutes each morning when you can be completely alone for what I call the faith period. The faith period is an important part of the total goal-setting and planning procedure. Without faith, no goal or plan would ever become reality. The Bible defines faith as *the confident assurance that something we want is going to happen. It's the certainty that what we hope for is waiting for us even though we cannot see it up ahead.* That's Hebrews 11:1.

Faith is what you have left after everything else has been lost. It's the most powerful motivating force in the world. Millions of people are looking to the future with great expectancy because of their faith. Wish and hope devoid of faith and belief are fruitless.

The faith period's sole purpose is to help you grow in faith, which in turn will enable you to do outstanding things. Let's get into the actual mechanics of how to conduct your own personal faith period.

The faith period should be very personal. Its purpose is to put you in tune with the great infinite, intelligent God of the universe. First, form the habit of becoming an early riser. There was a time in my life when I would set my alarm clock to sound just 30 minutes before I was required to be on my job. I would awaken, rush, rush, rush and arrive at my work totally and mentally unprepared to meet the opportunities and frustrations of the day. The early-morning hours set the stage for the activities of the day. If they are pleasant, the entire day will be pleasant. Today I arise each morning at 5:30 and slowly prepare myself for the day. I look forward to the day with the greatest expectancy that good things are going to happen. I drive to the office, arriving at 6:30. Going to the office at this hour of the day creates a tremendous feeling of power and authority. At that time of day you are probably the only person going to work because you want to. The others you see are going to work because they have to. You feel you are out in front of everyone else, and you are. You feel the world is yours for the taking. It is. You feel you can conquer any obstacle standing between you and your goal. You will. The Bible says, *"If you love sleep, you will end in poverty. Stay awake, work hard and there will be plenty to eat."* That's Proverbs 20:13.

I've also formed the habit of complimenting those with whom I come in contact in the early-morning hours. The compliments give others a tremendous boost for the day, but I benefit most of all, because giving compliments gives me inner happiness.

Resolve now to arise early, take your time and be a cheerful friend, and as a result you will have many friends. You're probably thinking there's no way you can rise early and be a cheerful friend. I'm a late sleeper. I once felt the same way. There's a price to be paid in the beginning. But once you form the habit, you will discover that your early-morning time and your faith period will be the most enjoyable and important time of the day. In the morning your mind is rested; it's not crammed with the thousand trivial details that fill it at the end of the day. You can do your most productive thinking in the morning. Become an early riser no matter what your present sleep habits may be.

When I arrive at my office, I begin my faith period. I sit in a comfortable chair and totally relax my entire body. Relaxation of the physical body frees the mind for deep meditation. I continue my faith period by reading the 91st Psalm, which includes these words: "*For the Lord says, because he loves me I will rescue him. I will make him great because he trusts in My name. When he calls on Me, I will answer. I will be with him in trouble and rescue him and honor him. I will satisfy him with a full life and give him My salvation.* You should not put your faith in a man. Put faith in God and His promises and you will have the strength to withstand any adversity." Ralph Waldo Emerson once said, "Alone, a man is sincere." The faith period is a time when you have the opportunity to be sincere with yourself. Everyone needs time alone with God daily. It helps you keep a proper perspective about life.

As I continue my faith period, I communicate with God. I imagine He is sitting in a chair in the room with me, and then I talk to Him through my thoughts. I imagine that He is not only the best and most loyal friend I've ever had, but also the wisest. He has all the answers. God is the one who forgives. If I have committed any sins I discuss them with Him, ask Him to forgive me. Next, I give thanks for all the good things that happened to me on the previous day. Then I express my concern for those I love, those in need, the sick, and those I resent. Next, my thoughts turn to my own personal needs, both problems and opportunities. Through my thoughts I petition for answers and results, claiming the promise that is mine in Mark 11:24: "*Listen to me, you can pray for anything and if you believe you have it it's yours." We're also given the promise, "Ask and you will be given what you ask for, seek and you will find, knock and the door will be opened."* That's Matthew 7:7 and 8.

After the meditation portion of the faith period has ended, program your mind by repeating your goals and plans. If you'll keep your goals before you each day, they are certain to become a reality. Repeating orders from your thinking mind to your subconscious mind will convert thoughts into reality. At this point, glance through your monthly and weekly activity planners to be sure that top-priority items and details have been written down. Transfer plans from your weekly planner to your daily planner and then take action. Make it happen. Design a faith period for yourself. Take 30 minutes to be alone each morning and follow an established procedure. If you do, your life will immediately change for the better, and within a 10 to 30-day period you will experience some remarkably good things. *"I will instruct you, says the Lord, and guide you along the best pathway for your life. I will advise you and watch your progress."* That's Psalm 32:8. You can do it if you have faith.

The man who is a master of human relations is priceless. Industry and business will richly reward the individual who can expertly achieve positive results through other people. In all my experience, I don't believe I've ever met more than a handful of men who were masters in the art of human relations. I've found, without exception, that men who possess this outstanding skill are men who are on their way to the top, or who have already reached the pinnacle of success. Why are men who master human relations so successful? Because they have learned and accepted a simple principle called the Golden Rule: Do for others what you want them to do for you. By enthusiastically applying the Golden Rule in your own life, you will enrich the lives of many others, but by far the greater reward will come to you. Good will radiated from you will be returned to you in the form of happiness and prosperity. The people you come in contact with will suddenly become members of your fan club. Treating others as you like them to treat you will cause them to do everything within their power to help you achieve your goals in life. You may meet someone who will not respond to this rule. If so, go the extra mile. Show them patience and understanding. Treat them exactly like the person you want them to be and they will do their best to become that person.

Now let's examine the portrait of a master of human relations:

1. He will seem simple, but is wise. The French author Modisque said, "I've always observed that to succeed in the world a man must seem simple, but be wise." If you appear to be a simple man, others will tend to underestimate your ability and will present you the opportunity to deal with them when their guard is down. By seeming simple, but being wise, you can accomplish your objectives before anyone actually realizes what is happened and yet everyone will be happy. Psalm 37:35 through 38 says, *"For the good man, the blameless, the upright, the man of peace, he has a wonderful future ahead of him. For him, there is a happy ending."*

2. He will be humble; he will be able to accept his achievements for their true worth and not as something that makes him better than others. He will possess control over his temper, because a quick temper affects his judgment and relations with others. The good shepherd said, *"For everyone who tries to honor himself shall be humbled. And he who humbles himself shall be honored."* That's Luke 14:11.

3. He will be genuinely interested in others. He will treat everyone with respect regardless of their social status, because he knows that everyone is a child of God and has a useful service to render to humanity. He is a man you can talk with. He will take time to listen, and he is able to offer you sound advice. He has the capacity to sincerely love his brother. Don't just pretend that you love others. Really love them. Hate what is wrong. Stand on the side of good. *Love each other with brotherly affection and take delight in honoring each other.* That's

Romans 12:9 and 10.

4. He'll be honest in business dealings and in his personal life. To succeed in working with people, you must be honest in every aspect of your life. In Romans 12:17 we find this statement, *"Do things in such a way that everyone can see that you are honest clear through. Leave no room for any doubt.* If your friends and business associates consider you to be an honest man, they'll entrust to you the big responsibilities regarding business and financial matters."

5. He'll not involve himself in gossip and slander. He realizes that malicious gossip is spread by people with small minds. *Any story sounds true until someone tells the other side and sets the record straight.* That's Proverbs 18:17. Idle gossip destroys others, and it will destroy you if you clutter your mind with it. If you can't say something good about a person, don't say anything.

6. He'll give credit and praise to others. One of the easiest ways to lose the loyalty and support of others is by taking credit for the accomplishment of objectives yourself. *"Don't praise yourself; let others do it."* That's Proverbs 27:2. This is difficult, but praise will come to you in abundance if you truly deserve it.

7. He will be patient and kind. The inexperienced don't understand the great power of having patience. They tend to want everything to happen yesterday. Benjamin Disraeli said, "Everything comes if a man will only wait. A human being with a settled purpose must accomplish it, and nothing can resist a will that will stay in existence for its fulfillment." Another important virtue is kindness. This characteristic will create an inner peace that can be found no other way. *"Your own soul is nourished when you are kind. It's destroyed when you are cruel."* That's Proverbs 11:17.

8.   He will be fair and just. Your associates and friends can accept almost anything you do if they feel they are being treated fairly. Present each individual an equal opportunity and then let their own efforts determine how happy and successful they'll become. A master of all human relations must also be just. He must gather all the facts, consider all the solutions, then make the best decision based on the facts and stick with it. If you treat others with justice, they will hold you in high regard. *The Lord demands fairness in every business deal.* That's Proverbs 16:11.

9.   He will give and accept constructive criticism. Constructive criticism has only one purpose: to help others. It should never be administered as a rebuke, but only as a means to arrive at solutions for adverse situations that occur to everyone who takes action. The only people who do not create problems are those who do nothing. The rest, the doers, must continually face problems each day. The master of human relations must be willing to listen to complaints, weigh them carefully in his thoughts, extract the truth and profit by them. *"Don't refuse to accept criticism. Get all the help you can."* That's Proverbs 23:12.

10.   He will be a decent person. He must strive every day to live within the boundaries of the laws of God. You will fail from time to time, but when you do, get back on track. King David, one of God's most beloved, was continually getting off the right track, but he was aware of his human weakness, and by admitting his mistakes put himself on the correct course. If others know that you are basically a sound person, they'll focus their attention upon the many good things you stand for. *The Lord blesses good men.* That's Proverbs 12:2.

11.   He will be generous with others. We're not referring to the word "generous" in the material sense. We refer to his

generosity in offering himself to others. He cannot allow
self to stand in the way. Others come first. Simply forget
about getting. *"Be generous, and give of yourself and all
goes well for the generous man who conducts his
business fairly."* That's Psalm 112:5.

12.   He will possess a positive mental attitude. This is a
      powerful magnet that will attract others. Learn to live in
      the expectation that good things are going to happen if
      you are to be a master of human relations. A positive
      mental attitude rubs off on others. Maintain a positive
      mental attitude and you'll go far in dealing with people.

One who possesses all 12 qualities will rise to great heights
during his life and will be long remembered after he returns to the
grave.

There are several other topics that should be discussed before
leaving the topic of human relations.

First, if you sincerely want to accomplish outstanding things,
you must surround yourself with capable helpers. You will be no
better or no more effective than the people around you. A head
football coach is no better than his assistant coaches, and the
president of a corporation is no better than his staff.

Another principle is that as you go to the top there will always
be inequalities. There will always be the corporate president who
promotes his 23-year-old son to vice president after only six
months of service. There will always be the guy who receives the
same raise you do when you've been doing all the work. There
will always be unfairness to face as long as there are people.
Don't get involved. Keep working toward your own personal
goal. Free yourself from all pettiness and prejudice, set your
sights on your personal goals and let no one stand in your way. It
takes character to keep forging ahead.

If you master the art of human relations, you can achieve
anything your heart desires, just by working through people. Take
time to find out what other people want, and spend your time
helping them to get it, and you will be successful. Remember, *do
to others what you want them to do to you.* You can be a master

of human relations if you believe you can.

You possess talents that are possessed by no other living creature. You need only to develop your talents and you will be well on your way to a lifetime of happiness and success. You possess these talents because you are a unique creation, the only one of your kind. It was planned that way by the Creator from the beginning. The useful services you can render are unique to you. You must search inside yourself to find those talents. Your talents will coordinate perfectly with your wants and desires once you discover them. Once you discover your talents and put them to work as a useful service for others, you'll be happy and successful because you will be doing the things you want to do and those are the things you do best. The Apostle Paul said, *"Don't copy the behavior and customs of this world, but be a new and different person with a fresh newness in all you do and think."* That's Romans 12:2.

Paul is saying, don't conform. Dare to be different and operate within the bounds of the great natural laws of the universe that were established by God. You have a spirit that will lead you to greatness and can mold your life so you will truly achieve your maximum potential. This spirit is available only to those who seek it. It is the spirit of the Creator. Regardless of your present circumstances, you can be happy and successful by taking complete control of your thoughts, and you can rise above your negative circumstances.

Throughout history few people have suffered greater adversity than Helen Keller. A serious illness destroyed her sight, hearing, and speech before she was two years old. She was entirely shut off from the world, living as a blind deaf mute. Her teacher, Ann Sullivan, made contact with the girl's mind through the sense of touch. Within three years Helen knew the alphabet and could read and write in Braille. In 1904 she graduated from Radcliffe with honors. She became a noted lecturer and author. Her best-selling books have been translated into more than 50 languages. It would have been very easy for Helen Keller to lose her faith and give up hope many times during her life. But she didn't, because she had realized that she was a child of God, a unique creation possessing an important service to render to mankind. Her love and concern for others gained her worldwide fame. She became a legend in her lifetime.

You probably don't have to overcome as great a degree of adversity as Helen Keller did to secure a happy and successful life. Your circumstances can be altered at any time you choose so that you may begin your journey toward inner peace, riches, enlightenment and physical well-being. Are you allowing your present circumstances to keep you from achieving your full potential as a person? If you are, you are wasting your God-given talents. If you have a genuine thirst for opportunity, then launch out confidently, leaving the details of providing for the necessities of life to the spirit within you. Jesus said, *"Your heavenly Father already knows perfectly well that you need them, and He will give them to you if you give Him first place in your life and live as He wants you to."* That's in Matthew 6:33.

If you have worthwhile goals and are going in the right direction, your needs will be provided for. If you are living within the boundaries of God's guidelines for mankind, He will meet all your needs. Too many people today feel unloved and unwanted. They are wrong. God cares for each of us with a perfect love, which is beyond human understanding. To Him you are very important. The psalmist instructs, *"it is better to trust the Lord than to put confidence in men."* That's Psalm 118:8.

Human love is imperfect, but the love of God is perfect. In Him you have a true friend. If you are His child, His spirit is within you. When you call upon Him He will be there. If you think you are not loved, forget it. You are so loved that Jesus gave His life for you. You need no other love than the one true love offered in great abundance by the one who really cares the most about you, the Creator of all. Fully realizing that you are a unique being with talents and services to offer and that you are deeply loved, it's time to explore the unlimited opportunities available to you.

Some people believe that opportunity knocks only for the rich and powerful. Some believe there is a fickle finger of fate that taps certain individuals on the shoulder and points them in the direction of wealth and power. Some believe that opportunity has passed them by. They don't believe that an individual is rewarded in direct proportion to the thought and effort he puts forth.

Just after graduation, two young friends asked a multi-millionaire about the chance of earning a million dollars. The old gentleman had little formal education, but he possessed a lot of common sense. My friends thought it more difficult to earn one million dollars today than ever before, and they gave many reasons to prove their point. Finally they asked the old man his opinion. "I think it is easier to earn a million dollars today than ever before," he said. "You boys have a problem, though. You went to college. College doesn't teach you how to strike out on your own, as I did when I was your age."

We must break the bonds of conformity and then use all our mental and physical resources to produce a lifetime of happiness and success. Observe the tremendous abundance all around you. Nature blossoms with unending beauty. Our Creator has provided for all the needs of nature. Drive through your city and consider the fantastic ingenuity and wealth required to construct skyscrapers and freeway systems.

As you observe the tremendous abundance around you, remember that you have as much right to that abundance as any other person. But it will not be given to you, it must be earned. Opportunity comes to those who seek it. Webster's Dictionary defines opportunity as a time or occasion that is right for doing something. The time or occasion will appear when you have mentally prepared yourself to recognize and receive it. To bring this opportunity to fruition requires doing something. Opportunity is everywhere. Most people don't recognize it for what it is, or they allow fear to cripple their thoughts of success.

An elderly man had been earning a meager living from a grocery business for more than 35 years and had reached retirement age. Because of inadequate retirement income, he was forced to enter life insurance selling as a new career. He was an immediate success. He repeatedly told me of the tremendous fulfillment he received from his work. His annual income was considerably more during retirement than during his peak earning years in the grocery business. He said he wished this opportunity had been available to him when he was younger. He never stopped to realize that this opportunity had been available when he was younger, but he had not taken time to discover it.

Francis Bacon, the English philosopher, wrote "A wise man will make more opportunities than he finds." You must make your opportunities if you want to enjoy a happy and successful life. God has provided everything you need to live a good life. You are exposed to exciting opportunities each day. To capitalize on them you must grasp only those opportunities that are in harmony with your ability to take advantage of them. You possess the spirit to be happy and successful, and you live in a world that provides you with unlimited opportunity. You are important, you are loved, you are a unique creation, and you have unlimited opportunity available because you live in a world governed by a God who knows no limitations. In God's world you can be great if you believe you can.

If you were going to live to be 800 years old, you could afford to waste three to four hundred years of your life doing unimportant things. But this is not the case. From the moment you draw your first breath you begin a personal race against time. Time is a precious jewel that must be guarded well and worn with discretion or you will suddenly realize that it has been stolen. If you use your time wisely and with respect, your life will be one of abundance. But if you neglect time, it will neglect you. You might have wasted yesterday, you may even be wasting today, but tomorrow is kept fresh and waiting for you. You can turn over a new leaf with each dawning day, if you choose. But don't delay. The proper use of time in your life will guarantee you happiness and success. Proverbs 10:4 tells us, *"Lazy men are soon poor, hard workers get rich."*

We live in an age of gross materialism. Increasing physical wealth is accompanied by a decline in spiritual values. There is a feeling that something is wrong. People express a feeling of emptiness and unrest. They want more leisure time. They want to work less and play more. Because so many are interested in getting more money for doing less, think how great the opportunity is for someone who is interested in giving more and providing better service to the people he serves, spending his time and energy and equipping himself to do a better job, learning to enjoy life fully as a thoroughly balanced individual and adding to his share of happiness.

Avoid materialism, and don't rest on your laurels once they are won. To continue prosperity, engage in worthwhile work and efficiently use your time. You can do this by having personal goals and plans. God said, "*Six days shalt thou labor and do all thy work.* By totally committing yourself to work you will be able to enjoy your leisure." In Ecclesiastes 11:4 we find another important key to becoming happy and successful, "*If you wait for perfect conditions you will never get anything done. Perfect circumstances will never come. Get on with your opportunity.*"

Many people resemble the little-known painter who planned a masterpiece. He described it in detail to friends many times as the years passed, but he never found the right times or conditions to begin painting. He took his masterpiece to the grave with him, for it lived only within him.

Don't reach the sunset of life having accomplished nothing worthwhile. Forget about your age, status, nationality or race. Decide what you really want from life and go after it. Action makes dreams become a reality. The vital elements of a happy and successful life are time, work and action. Time control combined with hard work and action, built on the firm foundation of belief, create a potent force.

The line has been drawn. If you step over it, you will have inner peace, riches, enlightenment and physical well-being. Taking that step means that you accept these principles. It also means you must put them to work in your life today.

Decide to take that step. As you begin to live in this happy and successful way, you will find that the floodgates of balanced living will open for you. Your view of your opportunities and the future will be overwhelming, and you will feel better than you have in many years. You will be among an exclusive minority who lead wonderfully happy and successful lives. Begin today; you have nothing to lose. But you have a happy and successful life to gain.

Almost 2000 years ago Jesus showed us the secret of success. Let His life be an example by which you will achieve happiness and success, and you cannot possibly fail. May the Creator bless you as He has me.

13

Personal Development Game Plan

INCOME SELDOM EXCEEDS PERSONAL development. There is a reason why homes costing over $250,000 have libraries. If you have no room for a library in your current home or you cannot afford to purchase books, you're in luck. Public libraries will actually allow you to borrow books free of charge! Imagine that. The only cost involved is taking the time to apply for a library card.

It's sad that only 3% of Americans own a library card. If you don't have one, run out and get one today. It's one of your keys to personal development if you're short on cash. The best advice I can give you is to begin reading, listening, and participating in seminars that will stimulate your personal development on a regular basis. Begin a new reading or listening habit today. Turn your car into a mobile classroom!

RECOMMENDED READING

Success! The Glenn Bland Method
The Power of Thought
One-Minute Student Bible
Legend of the Golden Scrolls
Think and Grow Rich
Think and Grow Rich: A Black Choice
The Templeton Plan
The Five Rituals of Wealth
The Richest Man in Babylon
The Living Bible

RECOMMENDED LISTENING

SUCCESS: The Glenn Bland Method audiobook
Jim Rohn's 2-Day Seminar on tape
Think and Grow Rich audio series

RECOMMENDED PARTICIPATION

2-Day Seminar by Jim Rohn, (800) 929-0434
Bible Study Fellowship, (210) 492-4676

Most of the books and audio cassettes listed above you will want to read and listen to over and over again. These are not just books you read once and put back on the shelf. Renewing your mind takes time.

14

How to Establish a
New Bank Relationship

IF YOU'RE LIKE ME, you've really never met a banker whom you truly liked. It started very young with me. I was an entrepreneur as a teen-ager. I wanted to be a professional photographer, and needed money to purchase photographic equipment. No bank would consider loaning money to me. Bank after bank would send me a decline letter. Ever since then I have always felt that bankers "didn't have a clue."

Well, when you meet the right banker it makes a world of difference. They're out there; just hard to find. There are bankers who really want to help you get re-established, and will do everything in their power to help you. Let's get started.

BANK VS. CREDIT UNION

This biggest problem I have against credit unions is that they usually do not report your timely loan payments to the credit reporting agencies.

So you may establish new credit with your credit union, but its not helping you since no other lender will see your timely payments! If you're using a credit union now, call up the branch manager and ask which of the three credit reporting agencies they report to. If they don't report, my advice would be to find one that does.

CHECK VERIFICATION SYSTEMS

When I first moved to Indianapolis I was quickly turned down while attempting to open a checking account with a certain bank.

It irritated me, even though I had a previous habit of writing checks that bounced. The history of my rubber checks showed up on various check-verification services. So how do you get around check-verification services? There are two ways.

The easiest way is to let your fingers do the walking in the Yellow Pages. Call each bank branch closest to you and ask some simple, yet direct, questions about opening a new account.

I found something really surprising: Not all banks subscribe a check-verification system. Especially the smaller banks. What's more, there are different check-verification systems!

I called and asked for the person in charge of opening new accounts. Once on the phone I introduced myself and said I was interested in opening checking and savings accounts. I asked the person to explain the most cost-effective account fees and minimum deposit requirements. It was also important to me to have a debit bank card, so I asked how I could obtain one and what the requirements were.

If everything seemed okay, I asked which check-verification system they used to open new accounts. If the person hesitated even slightly, I quickly responded that I had a few returned checks that might prevent me from opening an account.

After reviewing the notes I had taken on each call, I would then decide which bank I felt offered the most services for the money, and would visit the branch to open new accounts.

The second way is more fun. It involves paying attention to new bank branches in the area. New bank branches are eager to sign up new bank accounts, and they sometimes waive standard procedure in verifying accounts.

After my first attempt to establish a bank account failed, I tried again. While waiting for my wife at a job interview, I noticed three brand-new bank branches on the same corner of a fairly new part of town. I knew something special was going to happen.

I went into one of the banks and asked to speak to the person in charge of opening new accounts. As I was sitting down in his office, I told him I would like to open checking and savings accounts. I then proceeded to tell him that I might have a few returned checks on his bank's check-verification system and I was not sure whether they would accept me as a client.

His answer was, "No problem." Within 10 minutes I walked out of the bank with checking and savings accounts. No check-verification system was used.

So, if you're in a situation where you don't think you could get a bank account, let my story be an encouragement to you. Make it happen.

At this point I was so elated that we had a checking account again that it didn't matter that this banker wasn't interested in helping me re-establish credit. The important thing now was that with an existing bank account I could be more selective in choosing a long-term bank partner. Once you have a checking account, few bankers use their check-verification system to establish a new account. Bankers love it when you switch to their bank from a competitor. In fact, some banks give you a special bonus for being a new customer.

Remember, you can always pay any outstanding checks listed on the check-verification system. This will help you if the banks in your area all subscribe to the same system. I would recommend you pay these anyway to avoid future problems.

FINDING A GOOD BANKER

How I found my good bankers was through referrals and by hard work on the telephone. In this case two referrals came from people working for organizations extending micro-loans to low-income people within the community. The other was a result of a telephone survey of bankers in the area.

My logic was that anyone dedicated to helping low-income people rehabilitate their lives would be connected to people who might be able to help me.

It is not easy finding a good banker. If you find a good banker who helps you, please forward his or her name and address to us. If you have the time and energy to locate your own good banker, the place to start is on the telephone.

(1)   Start with your existing bank branch
(2)   Call your bankruptcy attorney and ask for a referral
(3)   Call bank branch managers directly

The time and effort you put into finding your good banker is worth its weight in gold. Having a good banker will accelerate your ability to obtain mainstream credit.

GO WHERE THE GOOD BANKER IS

Our bankers are 30 minutes or more away from our house. In fact, I pass at least 10 other banks while driving to their location. Where your banker is located should not matter. You simply open accounts with your good banker and do your regular business with branches that are closest to you. Having a banker who is willing to help you is more important than how close the bank is to your home.

My friend David didn't see the importance of working with a banker who was willing to help him re-establish credit. He decided to ask the bank manager closest to him to do the same things my banker would do. Not only was the banker not willing to help, but she told my friend that it couldn't be done. What's interesting is that it was the same bank, just a different branch.

This happens a lot. Don't be discouraged if one branch manager says no. The next one you talk with may be very open to work with you. It's a matter of personality and experience.

WHAT MAKES A GOOD BANKER?

A good banker will provide several important things as you begin your journey back to financial stability:

1. A secured bank loan using the loan proceeds as the collateral. This avoids having to put up the loan amount as collateral
2. Free checking and savings accounts
3. Minimum checking-account activation deposit of $25
4. Checks starting at higher number instead of 001
5. An automatic approval of a Visa debit bank card
6. No charge to use their ATM
7. The high probability of receiving overdraft protection within six months to a year

A good banker is usually someone in authority, like a branch manager. Someone without authority will not help you in the long term. Don't waste your time with anyone other than a top manager.

Bob, one of my favorite bankers, is so good that he has moved to four different branches since I've known him. I will move my accounts wherever he goes. It pays to go where the good banker is. You are building a relationship with a person, not an image or a television campaign.

One of my new bankers, Tom, is also very good. He was responsible for my recent overdraft-protection account of $2,500. We'll be with Tom for a long time.

Sometimes one banker can't do it all. You may need a few of them. Bob couldn't get me an unsecured overdraft-protection account, but Tom could. Just go with the flow.

WHAT TO EXPECT FROM YOUR GOOD BANKER

The most important thing a good banker can do for you is help you re-establish your credit by means of a secured bank loan. There are two types of secured bank loans. The first one requires you to put up the amount of loan in cash as collateral before they will loan you money. The second type only good bankers do. It's still a secured loan, but the loan is secured by the loan proceeds, so you do not need to put up the initial cash to get the loan.

Most bankers won't even do the secured bank loans, let alone the kind where you use the loan proceeds as collateral.

My good banker set me up with several secured bank loans without initial cash. I decided to visit a few other banks and do the same thing. Most of them couldn't understand what I wanted to do. In fact, when I did find one that would give me a secured loan, they would not use the loan proceeds as collateral.

Remember that these people are doing a specific job. To most of them it is just a job, that's all. They don't really care about your needs or special concerns. A good banker will do everything he or she can do to help you.

This is what to ask for. Tell them you have a previous bankruptcy and want to re-establish credit. Tell them the best way for you to do that is by getting a secured bank loan. Ask them whether their bank approves secured loans. If you get a yes, ask whether they can use the loan proceeds as collateral so you will not have to put up your own money. You may have to repeat yourself slowly a few times. Uncreative bankers need to hear it more than one time to understand it.

So how does a secured loan work? After you find a banker who is willing to do one, it's pretty simple. First you need open checking and savings accounts. Usually you can open these accounts with $25 to $50, depending on the individual bank. After you have bank accounts you need to fill out a loan application. The banker should know your previous history before you submit a credit application. Use the methods outlined in previous chapters to help you prepare. Once approved, it's all a matter of signing paperwork. Some banks can approve them the same day, while others require you to come back the next day. It depends on that particular bank's policy. The bank then deposits the loan proceeds (or check) you sign over to them into a savings account, and places a hold on that account. This hold means you will be unable to withdraw funds put on hold. Other than that, it's a regular savings account. If you default, the loan is completely secured. Within a week or so you will receive a bank loan payment book in the mail. You start making monthly payments on your loan. When you pay off the loan, the money you saved belongs to you. Think of it as a forced savings account.

Another hidden benefit of the secured bank loan is the savings account. Now you can honestly write on any credit application that you have so many thousand dollars in a savings account in your bank. The lender can even call and verify to find it to be true.

Getting a secured bank loan without using the loan proceeds as collateral works the same way, except that you must put up the loan amount in cash. These are no fun. Bankers who have no creativity do this kind of loan. Keep looking for a banker who is concerned more about you.

There are creative banks, like First of America Bank, that have specific secured-loan programs. Their program is called "Credit Builder." You deposit $200 for every $1,000 loan you would like, and they make a secured loan for you. It's a great program that more banks should have.

The second thing a good banker can do for you is provide no-fee bank checking and savings accounts. With the monthly fees on checking accounts averaging $15 a month, this becomes an important issue to someone trying to save money.

Most customer-oriented banks have a program whereby if you have so much money in savings with them they will waive all normal bank maintenance fees. This is the kind of bank you want to work with. Most banks have these programs. Having just received a bank loan, this should qualify you to receive no-fee accounts. I recommend obtaining a secured loan amount that would qualify you to have all bank fees waived. Ask before you decide on the loan amount. At my bank, having $1,000 in savings qualifies you for no-fee bank accounts.

The third thing a good banker can do for you is allow you to open your new checking and savings accounts with the minimum amount. Every bank has a different policy, but most will allow you to start a new account with $25. The amount varies from state to state. The most I have ever opened an account with was $100 in Chicago. Simply ask what the minimum deposit is to open an account.

The fourth thing a good banker will do for you is allow to start your checks at a higher number than 001. You will likely be hassled by merchants over a low check number wherever you go, so be sure to remember to ask for this when your placing your check order. Some banks have a policy limiting the number for new accounts. If that's the case, open an account but do not order checks from them. There are other companies you can purchase checks from that allow you to have any check number you want; in addition, the cost of the checks is usually half what the banks charge. A company you can order checks from is:

Current Checks
P.O. Box 19000
Colorado Springs, CO 80935
(800) 204-2244

Rather than ordering through the bank and paying more for your checks, go directly to the printer. The only difference is that your bank logo will not appear in the lower left corner of your checks. Instead, your bank name will be in type.

On first orders with these companies you must mail in your order. It's kind of inconvenient, but re-orders can be handled over the telephone. It's worth the hassle to get a higher-starting check number.

The fifth thing a good banker will do for you is automatically approve you for a Visa debit card. These are good to have when you are just starting out. It works just like a normal Visa or MasterCard, except that instead of accessing a line of credit, the money comes out of your checking account.

For several years these debit cards were just as hard to get as a normal bank card. Bankers have finally awakened to understand that they save money when their customers use electronic debit transactions to pay for things, versus writing checks. Now most of the larger banks are adapting new policies that push debit cards.

The biggest benefit for me in using my debit card is how fast payments post to the account. For instance, I could make a deposit at 12:15 in the afternoon, and as I am pulling out of the bank I can be on the cellular telephone with a supplier with my debit card number to place an order. It's fast. Or if I went out of town on business, my wife could deposit money into the account for me to access very quickly, compared to mailing a payment and waiting up to a week to post.

The sixth thing a good banker provides is waiving the service fees for using their ATM machines. Those small fees add up to a small fortune over a period of time. My wife and I refuse to pay ATM service fees. We will either drive to use one of our bank's machines or visit our local grocery store, which cashes personal checks. Only in emergencies do we use an ATM machine that charges us a service fee. Most banks do not charge when you use their own ATM machines.

The seventh thing a good banker will do is slowly trust you with unsecured lines of credit. It may start with overdraft protection consisting of a few hundred dollars connected to your checking account.

The important thing to remember is that it takes time to get to the place where you can get unsecured credit with banks, even if your salary has tripled since your bankruptcy. My wife and I have now had re-established credit for almost six years, and we have only recently begun to go after unsecured credit through traditional channels.

Do not expect to be able to qualify for unsecured credit immediately after you finish paying off your first secured bank loan. Just keep credit active and pay your bills early or on time. Always be on the lookout for new good bankers. Your patience will pay off. Keep a good attitude and your time will come. Besides, if you're doing everything right, you won't need the unsecured lines of credit, they will only be a convenience.

I repeat: If you have found a good banker who is creative, please forward the person's name and address so we can include them in our database to share with others. You will be helping people save the time to look. Good luck, and most of all, have fun!

15

How to Get Approved for a Major Bank Card

MAJOR BANK CARDS ARE an important ingredient in re-establishing credit after bankruptcy. Bank cards are credit cards issued through Visa and MasterCard. But is it really necessary to have a bank card?

There are many valid reasons to carry a bank card. But most important is that lenders like to see a bank card on your credit report, with a history of timely payments.

It's also a matter of convenience. When was the last time you tried to make hotel reservations without a bank card? Or rented a car while on vacation? Or purchased airline tickets? There are people who make the majority of their purchases over the telephone to save time. Others appreciate the convenience of having an itemized bill every month.

The three lesser-known benefits of bank cards are liability, fraud protection, and purchase protection.

Liability is the most powerful reason to carry bank cards. Unlike its twin, the debit card, a bank card offers protection to the consumer under the Fair Credit Reporting Act (FCRA) for any liability over $50. Not so with debit cards or business bank cards. In fact, you may be responsible for the whole amount.

If you accidentally get involved with a company that defrauded you, the chances of getting your cash back are pretty slim. But by using your bank card, a credit for the purchase is just a phone call away. The bank does everything for you!

Purchase protection is a value-added perk that is available on some cards that guarantee the items you purchase from theft, accidental breakage, etc.

UNSECURED BANK CARDS

So how can you qualify for unsecured bank cards? You don't, at least in the beginning. Any unsecured bank cards you receive will be through the "hit-or-miss" method.

There have been people who attend our seminars who have been approved for unsecured bank cards after bankruptcy by using the "hit-or-miss" method.

They fill out and mail in a bank card application they receive in the mail, say a prayer, and cross their fingers. Sometimes the bank card issuer makes mistakes. They either neglect to pull a credit report, or someone is sick that day, or the application reviewer makes a mistake. Mistakes do not happen often.

I do not recommend that you apply for unsecured bank cards using the "hit-or-miss" method. It is not worth the risk of a credit inquiry on your credit report, or the rejection you experience from a declined.

And be very skeptical of unsecured-bank-card schemes. My friend Steve recently told me of an advertisement he noticed in the local newspaper for an unsecured bank card. I wasn't interested in obtaining new credit with an unknown bank, but was curious as to what they were up to. This company advertises in newspapers, guaranteeing a low-limit unsecured bank card. All you need to do is participate in a local seminar in your area.

The bottom line was that they were more interested in selling you merchandise. Steve walked out halfway through the seminar after they began talking about their merchandise catalogs. There is no free ride—except at *our* seminars! Stop wasting your time and energy looking for something that doesn't exist. Begin with a secured bank card.

SECURED BANK CARDS

Secured bank cards are the way to go. They work like any other major bank card. The only difference is that your deposit equals your line of credit. Some banks require as little as $100 to get started, others $250, and still others $400 or more.

The good news is that with an excellent payment history, most secured cards will turn into an unsecured bank card within a short period of time—as early as 12 months, but usually within 18 months. Each secured-bank-card company is different. That is why it's important to ask questions.

The major complaint from people about unsecured bank cards is that the credit limits are so low that it doesn't seem to be worth their time and effort. Nothing could be farther from the truth. Be responsible over little, and you will be trusted with much. Remember, you have to prove that your bad money-management habits have disappeared.

There is one drawback to having low limits on a bank card. It's known as the authorization problem. Hotels are especially known for this. Let's say you check into a hotel in Manhattan with a room rate of $250 and you plan to stay for two days. The hotel may authorize your bank card for the entire $500, plus and additional $200 to cover dining, long-distance calls and snack bar purchases. This could be a problem if your limit is only $600. These situations can usually be worked out in advance. Call and ask their policy and be aware of this potential challenge.

Most of the direct-mail solicitations you receive from bank card companies are not for you. The last thing you want is a bank card from a company that is known to issue cards to people with poor credit. Find a shoebox and "file" all credit solicitations there until a later date.

A lot of secured-bank-card companies report your bank card as "secured" on your credit reports. Avoid companies with this policy. You don't want lenders to know you have secured cards. Your goal is to appear like someone who never had credit problems. Companies with this policy are more interested in their well-being than yours. They don't care and do not understand what you're trying to do. Move on to the next lender.

Our story in obtaining a secured bank card is interesting. I quickly found out that it was necessary for our bankruptcies to be discharged before applying. So I was ready the day we received our discharge letters in the mail. In fact, our first application went out the same day we received the discharge letter.

We really couldn't afford to deposit $400 to begin our first secured bank card only three months after bankruptcy. So to come up with the money, we each put in extra hours at work, sold unnecessary items around the house, returned things for credit, ate very light, and saved every dollar we could. My wife fought me every step of the way. I usually listen to her, but she couldn't see the big picture. She still saw credit as the enemy. My logic was, the longer we waited to re-establish credit, the longer it would take to recover. So don't wait six months before making application; that's six months you could have behind you as part of your payment history. It's best to start as soon as possible.

The company we chose, American Pacific Bank, guaranteed that we would have our card within two weeks of mailing in the application. This was very important to us, since we would probably need to use it immediately after receiving it. Sure enough, in exactly 14 days we had our first major bank card.

Eighteen months later our account was purchased by Orchard Bank. They've been very good to us. We now have three bank cards with Orchard Bank each with a credit limit between $2,700 and $3,000. Our Bank One bank card has a limit of $7,000.

WHAT TO LOOK FOR IN A SECURED BANK CARD

Before selecting a secured bank card provider, you need to ask a lot of questions. Every bank has its' own standards. So get on the telephone and start asking questions. Here are some things to consider before you choose a bank card.

WILL THEY ACCEPT YOU WITH A PREVIOUS BANKRUPTCY?

A basic question. But guess what—some secured-bank-card programs do not accept people with a bankruptcy. Go figure. They require that your bankruptcy be discharged. This you can easily support by mailing a copy of the discharge letter you received in the mail from the bankruptcy court.

IS THERE AN APPLICATION FEE?

Avoid any bank card provider with an application fee. The best bank cards do not require one. Companies that ask for an application fee are usually the companies that specialize in approving bank cards for uncreditworthy individuals. Do not waste your time, money, or effort with these companies. They are not your long-term players. You do not need to pay an application fee just because you filed bankruptcy.

WHAT IS THE MINIMUM INITIAL DEPOSIT REQUIRED TO OPEN AN ACCOUNT?

The minimum amount of your initial deposit varies from bank to bank. I have seen initial deposits as low as $100 and as high as $5,000. It is usually better to deposit as much as you can in the beginning, but if it's impossible for you to come up with the additional money, start immediately where you can. Some of the better bank card programs will double, even triple your initial deposit up to $5,000 depending on your credit score.

WHICH CREDIT BUREAUS DO THEY REPORT TO?

Very important question. What good is it if they will not report your excellent payment history to the credit bureaus? Bank card companies should report to the three major credit reporting agencies (Equifax, TransUnion and Experian), but there are many that choose not to.

OUT-OF-STATE CUSTOMERS

Not all bank card providers accept out-of-state customers. They may subscribe to only one of the major credit reporting agencies, or have a policy to stay within a certain area. Be sure to ask.

DO THEY REPORT YOUR SECURED BANK CARD AS SECURED?

Critical question. Simply ask whether they will report your secured card as secured on your credit reports. You want people to think they're unsecured. Do not accept an "I don't think so" answer. You must know beyond a shadow of a doubt. If the answer you receive is not an energetic "NO," ask for a supervisor. Be sure to write down his or her full name, direct telephone number, and the time and date for future reference. If it's their company policy to report secured cards as secured on credit reports, you have no need to continue the conversation. Thank them for their time and move on to the next call.

HOW QUICKLY DO THEY APPROVE?

The most common is three to four weeks. However, it is possible to receive one in seven to 14 days. Our first secured bank card arrived in exactly 14 days. Our next bank card, with the help of FedEx, arrived the same week! If you're in a hurry, mention that you're planning a vacation and would really like the convenience of their bank card. Notice that I said *planning* a vacation. I am not advocating lying. You can plan a vacation without ever going on one. Ask if they have a different address to send applications via overnight mail. Priority Mail is inexpensive ($3) and is guaranteed in two to three days. If a tracking number is important to you FedEx two-day service is good. It will put you on the top of the "normal" mail applications. Some may charge you for rush service; if you can afford the additional charge, it may be worth it for you.

HOW LONG UNTIL IT TURNS
INTO AN UNSECURED CARD?

The discipline is easier when you can see the end in sight. Choose a bankcard provider that specifically states how long before it turns into a unsecured card. The best programs are 12 to 18 months. Anything beyond that is too long.

What usually happens is that you have the option to keep your deposit invested and have your credit limit doubled, or request that your deposit funds be returned to you and retain the same credit limit, although unsecured.

Ask what things, other than late payments, would negatively affect your credit standing with them. Each lender is different. One lender may perceive going over your limit a negative mark; another would ignore it if it was paid before the next statement was issued. Just ask, and they will tell you.

If you do not establish an excellent payment history during the secured time period, the bank may delay or decline your bank card from converting into an unsecured card. So your question should be, "If I pay on a timely basis as agreed, when might I expect my card to be converted into an unsecured card?"

Some lenders issue a new bank card when your card converts into a unsecured card. All our bank card lenders issued us new cards. This is good. Another credit reference is added to your credit report. The more positive references on your credit report, the better.

HOW MUCH OF YOUR DEPOSIT IS AVAILABLE?

Not all banks will allow you to use the full amount you send in as a security deposit. But most will. Just make a point of knowing what your credit limit is before you begin to use it. However, there are some banks that automatically give you more credit than your security deposit.

Our first cards allowed us full benefit to the entire deposit amount. Our second card froze $100 of the security deposit. Within six months, however, they reapplied the amount to our limit after seeing a perfect payment history.

TOLL-FREE CUSTOMER SERVICE

This may not be important to you, but for us it was. We constantly call to hear our available limit and payments received. At times we would call the automated information line several times a day, usually just before eating out or going to the movies. Nothing is more embarrassing than standing in front of a long line of people and having your bank card denied. We always called first before making a purchase when our balance was close to the limit. It was close to the limit a lot in the beginning. If each long-distance call had cost us 50 cents, we would have easily spent $30 a month on long distance.

Our first bank card gave us toll-free access to the customer assistance center and long-distance access to the automated information line. When our bank cards were purchased by a larger bank 18 months later, we gained toll-free access to everything. Toll-free access may not be as important to you. Only you know your spending habits.

AUTOMATED ASSISTANCE?

Do they offer an automated assistance line, or do you have to speak with a person each time you call? The benefit of the automated attendant line is that you can call 24 hours a day. You can verify whether payments were received, what has posted to your account, what is pending, and your available credit, among other things.

INTEREST RATE

Frankly, the interest rate isn't very important right now. More important are the above benefits as a card holder. Expect to pay 15% to 21% for any bank card. Over time this will go down.

A few months after our cards converted into unsecured cards, I called to tell customer service that I was considering switching banks. They responded by lowering my interest rate on the spot, and at the same time increased my credit limit.

Accept any interest rate, within reason. Obviously, I would not pay anything over 21%. Ask when you might expect the interest rate to go down. The best times to ask are when your card converts to an unsecured card or during the holidays. Most secured-card lenders are having a tough time holding onto their customers after they turn into unsecured lines of credit. In fact, what a lot of lenders are doing is "selling" good accounts to larger banks that will allow lower interest rates, more benefits, and higher credit limits. This is good. The more positive credit references on your credit report, the better.

MAXIMUM DEPOSIT AMOUNT

Most secured cards will limit the amount of money you can put into them. The maximum is usually $5,000. One bank card company I know will triple your initial deposit amount if your credit score is high enough. So if you deposited $2,500, you may receive a $5,000 line of credit.

UNSECURED LIMIT LOOPHOLE

This is exciting. So exciting that I have saved the best for last. A few banks are really interested in helping you re-establish credit. They do this by providing an opportunity. The opportunity is a higher unsecured line of credit. Timing is everything when taking advantage of this loophole. To best explain it I will again draw from personal experience.

It all started when the customer assistance center of our bank card company informed me of a neat way of getting a higher unsecured limit. If I paid as agreed for 12 months I could then call and request to be reviewed for an unsecured card. The best part about it was that the unsecured credit limit became whatever the security deposit was at the time on the secured card. So this meant that if my bank card's maximum deposit amount was $5,000, in theory, I could automatically qualify for a $5,000 unsecured bank card in 12 months. All I had to do was figure out a way to save an additional $4,500 in 12 months. The opportunity had presented itself!

We tried very hard to increase our credit limit by sending in additional deposit amounts over the 12-month period, but it was obvious we were not committed to do it. What we decided to do was apply for a home equity loan and use $4,500 of the loan proceeds to increase our secured bank card limit before we requested that they review the account for unsecured status.

We sent the bank a $4,500 cashier's check via Priority Mail. We waited four or five days, then verified the payment posted to the account, using the automated information line. We then called to request that our secured bank card with a $5,000 secured line of credit be reviewed for unsecured status.

It worked. In less than one week we:

1.   were approved for a unsecured bank card
2.   were approved for a $5,000 unsecured line of credit
3.   had the $5,000 security deposit plus interest returned to us in the form of a certified check
4.   were extended a new account number, which meant

another positive reference on our credit file
5.   and the bank lowered our interest rate to 9.9% interest

We had no clue how we were going to come up with the $4,500. We knew it might be tough. We were already saving close to 30% of our income. Our responsibility was to believe it would happen, and it did.

So you're saying you don't want a $5,000 line of credit. Fine. What about $2,500? Decide what amount is comfortable to you and proceed.

It's a real convenience for us now. We can decide to take a vacation and just go. We don't need to call to see if there is enough credit available. When the bill comes, we pay it off. It's been a real blessing.

The question to ask is simple. Something like:

"...When I pay as agreed over x months, and I increase my credit limit to x dollars, how will you determine what my unsecured credit limit will be if I am approved?..."

Most telephone operators will not have a clue what you're talking about, so be prepared for their best guess. It's important that you get a solid answer here, so ask for a supervisor.

When I first learned about this trick I didn't believe it. I called back at least 10 to 15 times over 12 months just to be sure the person on the other end was telling the truth.

What they didn't tell me was to wait until the last minute and make a large deposit into my account, wait a few days, request a review for unsecured status, and look for my $5,000 back in less than seven days. This we figured out on our own. In fact, I'm convinced my bank changed their policy because of me. They now cap the unsecured limit to $2,500. Other banks do not.

Can you see that the benefits of the right bank card become more important than quibbling over an interest rate? Keep your eyes open and look for every opportunity. Sometimes all it takes is a friendly voice and a sincere interest in the other person.

CREDIT LINE INCREASES

It's easy to forget, since it's so simple. Most banks are on a six-month credit limit increase cycle. This means that you can call every six months and expect a credit line increase if you have paid as agreed.

As I began writing this paragraph I called my bank and asked for my credit limit to be increased. They asked me a few basic questions, and within a few minutes my credit line went from $5,000 to $7,000. I call it my $2,000 telephone call. All because I remembered to ask. I then proceeded to write in my day planner six months ahead to call the bank and request another credit increase.

Why is it important to always increase your credit limits? Because other lenders make their credit decisions based on compensating balances. For example, if my highest credit limit were $500, and I asked for a $2,000 loan, the chances of getting it would be slim. This is because my other credit limits were not at the same level of my request.

It's sort of like wanting to lease a Mercedes Benz, but you can only afford a Yugo. So keep increasing those credit limits. It makes getting credit approval on your next purchase that much easier.

BANK CARD RECOMMENDATIONS

Currently there are nearly 70 banks that offer secured-bank-card programs. I monitor them all on a quarterly basis. Out of those 70 secured programs, I recommend only two.

If you purchased this book at a seminar, you probably received an application from what I consider to be the best secured-bank card company in the country. If you purchased this book via mail order, an application was shipped with your book. If you purchased our book in a bookstore, please call us. We would be glad to direct you to the bank card that best meets your needs.

So why not just list the best bank card programs? Because they change constantly. In addition, there are different cards for different people.

For instance, one bank will not take people with a tax lien on their credit report; others will. One bank offers business bank cards. Another has a program for people in the military. Some offer initial deposits as low as $100. There are even banks that offer bank cards to people with no income. With others you need an initial deposit of several hundred. There are many programs to choose from.

16

6 Ways to Mortgage a Home After Bankruptcy

THERE ARE MANY WAYS to mortgage a home after bankruptcy. We'll discuss six of the most popular in this chapter.

1. Wait 24 months
2. Sub-prime lenders
3. First-time home buyer programs
4. Land contract conversion
5. 20% or more down payment
6. FHA Assumable No-Qualification

WAIT 24 MONTHS

After your bankruptcy has been discharged for 24 months, you can qualify for FHA or conventional financing. It gets better. Your interest rate may be the same as someone with a good credit rating.

I wish I could say you will "automatically" qualify. This depends on what you've done since the bankruptcy, and the lender's guidelines. Improve your chances of being approved by doing the following:

1. Establish at least three new credit accounts since your bankruptcy.
2. Stick with "mainstream" credit lenders.
3. Pay your bills early or on time.
4. Have no outstanding tax liens or levies reporting to the credit bureaus.
5. Have employment in the same line of work.

6.   Be able to afford the mortgage payment.
7.   The deal must make sense. Is your new mortgage payment lower than your current rent?

While you're waiting, be sure you keep in contact with the mortgage professional you have chosen to work with. This is important. Too many people assume things, and then when it's time to make application for a mortgage they don't qualify. The above list is just a starting point. A good mortgage professional will tell you what needs to be done and help you along the way.

This is a good example of why it's important to quickly re-establish credit after bankruptcy. Chances are there will be a time in the future when you need to borrow money—if not for yourself, for your children. No credit history, no new loan.

After a lender determines when your discharge date is, their next question will be how you've paid your bills since the bankruptcy. Late payments will cost you. Then a lender will ask what new credit you've established since the bankruptcy. Living on a cash-only basis does not impress them. Have at least three new lines of credit. The last major question will be how much money can you put down. A down payment can range from 1% to 5% of the purchase price of the home.

The type of credit you establish after your bankruptcy is important. It will determine how quickly you recover.

A student in our first bankruptcy seminar complained that he couldn't re-establish mainstream credit. I asked him some questions about his current credit accounts. All of it was paid as agreed. The problem was that none of it was mainstream credit. It was all high-interest credit. Be very careful what type of credit you attract after bankruptcy. You will receive more of what you attract.

Remember when you were back in high school for a moment. Who did the "druggies" hang out with? Other druggies. Who did the "popular" kids hang with? Other popular kids. You get the idea. The same goes for credit. You must avoid any credit that doesn't qualify as being mainstream credit.

Focus on re-establishing credit for a house, cars, major bank cards, business loans, home equity loans, and bank loans.

Department store credit is okay, just don't overdo it. Choose one or two stores. Avoid high-interest companies, buy-here-pay-here, rent-to-own, and finance companies.

Don't expect to qualify for a mortgage with only one small new credit reference since the bankruptcy, even if you were never late. Chances are it won't happen. You need to give lenders more assurance that you can pay your bills on time. You do that by opening at least three new lines of credit.

One deal-killer is late payments since the bankruptcy. My friend Steve was turned down for a mortgage for that reason. When he lived in Illinois he forgot to include the utility companies in his bankruptcy. They now reflect negatively on his credit report. Steve had an excellent income, enough time on the job, a mutual-fund account, a small bank loan, and a small bank card credit limit. The bottom line: mainstream lenders do not like late payments after a bankruptcy.

Lenders also do not like tax liens or tax levies on a credit report. Most lenders require them to be paid or subordinated if you want to re-finance or pull equity out. They're more lenient on a new purchase if you have an installment agreement with the I.R.S. and have paid on time for at least six months. Try re-establish credit before any tax liens or levies are put on your credit reports.

You should also have at least two years of employment in the same line of work. FHA only requires three to six months of employment. If you're job hopping, stay put until the day you close your mortgage.

Your debt-to-income ratio will determine whether you can afford the mortgage. This simply means the ratio of your debt to your income. For example, if you earn $2,000 a month and you spend $1,000 a month, your debt-to-income ratio will be 50%.

There are several ways to calculate your debt to income ratio. The most popular way is to figure it on a monthly basis and not include current rent, utilities or taxes. This was discussed in an earlier chapter.

Mortgage lenders like to see a debt to income ratio of no more than 28% on FHA mortgage loans. Conventional mortgages will go no higher than 36%. Keep this in mind as you plan your next move.

Waiting 24 months after your discharge date is your best choice. This gives you time to save money and re-establish mainstream credit. But you may not be in a position to wait. In that case, you need a sub-prime lender.

SUB-PRIME LENDERS

A relatively new breed of mortgage lenders will lend money to people who do not meet the qualifications for conventional or FHA mortgages, at a slightly higher interest rate. I'm not talking about high-interest finance companies here. I'm talking about mortgage companies that specialize in sub-prime credit. It's also known as B, C, D or alternative lending. If the deal makes sense, sub-prime lending could be a good option for you.

How do you know if the deal makes sense? Let's say you're currently paying $750 in rent each month. If a mortgage through a sub-prime lender will be lower than rent, it would make sense to me.

Not all sub-prime lenders are created equal. Each of them has a different program. You can easily spot them in the Yellow Pages. Read their ads. Look for "B, C, D credit" and "bankruptcy okay." Call them and inquire what kind of programs they have. Be careful. Many sub-prime lenders have one goal: charge you as much as possible.

Some companies that have sponsored our Credit After Bankruptcy Seminar® have loan programs with less than 5% down and interest rates close to grade conventional lenders.

Ask whether the lender will automatically refinance your mortgage into a conventional rate once you reach 24 months after discharge. If they will, you've found a good mortgage company.

Be sure to ask how much they will charge you to do your loan and how long it will take to close. Get everything in writing.

FIRST-TIME HOME BUYER PROGRAMS

There are many programs available to help you purchase a home. A good place to start is your state housing authority. See the Appendix for a partial list of housing authorities in the United

States. The best thing to do is call and tell them you want to talk to someone about becoming a homeowner.

My mother recently received a mortgage using one of these programs. After my father died a few years ago, she was forced to live with her sister for six months, we encouraged her to mortgage her own home. She earns less than $1,200 a month working part-time at the local hospital.

The state of Indiana has a program that helped her with the down payment. A wonderful program. All she had to do was come up with around $1,000 to close. Her mortgage payment is now less than what she would pay for rent.

She has told several of her widowed friends about the program. They also have become homeowners. Anything is possible if you believe.

LAND CONTRACT CONVERSION

If you have tax problems, chances are your only option until the taxes are paid will be a land contract. I know, I've been there. Our first house was a land-contract deal, because of unresolved tax problems.

Land-contract conversions are something new. It's where a Realtor and a mortgage company team up and put a marginal home buyer into a short-term land contract for 6 to 12 months, then, with an excellent payment history, move them into a mortgage on the same home.

Your best contact here is a Realtor. Creative Realtors will have a few of their own "listings" where deals like this may be possible. If not, they should know who does.

A land contract may have some of the same benefits as a mortgage. Every state is different. Ask your Realtor about the difference between a land contract and a mortgage in your state.

20% OR MORE DOWN PAYMENT

This may be out of reach for most of you. But it's true. If you have a large down payment, you are guaranteed to find a willing mortgage lender to lend you the money. Even mortgage companies with strict policies about lending to previous bankrupts will open their doors.

Let's say, for example, that you wanted to mortgage a home valued at $100,000. Using this method, you would need $20,000 to put down on this home to qualify for the mortgage.

Think about it. If you default, they have 20% or more equity within a tangible asset that they know how to sell. Banks understand how to sell homes in case of default. As long as the value of the home can be substantiated, you have a great chance of getting a mortgage.

Where the down payment comes from is an important consideration. It's best if it comes from an inheritance, savings, selling assets like cars or stocks, receiving an insurance settlement, or simply an outright gift. The more you have to put down, the easier it is to receive mainstream financing.

FHA ASSUMABLE NO-QUALIFICATION MORTGAGE

The no-qualifying assumption mortgage is perfect for people who have some money to put down and the ability to make a monthly payment, but cannot credit qualify for a mortgage using traditional methods.

The Federal Housing Administration (FHA) is a government entity that was created in 1934 to insure mortgages in response to the Great Depression. There have been over 15 million homes covered by FHA-insured mortgages since its inception.

The general idea was to make housing more affordable to a greater number of people by having the federal government insure the mortgage, even though the money itself was and is loaned by commercial banks and S&Ls.

Buying a home using FHA financing is generally a good idea even today, since the credit standards are a little easier, but mostly because of a lower down-payment requirement. Where most banks require 5% down, FHA requires only 3%.

The FHA is no longer insuring mortgages with a no-qualifying assumption. It stopped insuring them in December 1986. So any no-qualifying assumptions you find will be mortgaged before December 1986. After that, they can be assumed, but it will require credit approval.

No-qualify mortgages are everywhere. With 15 million of

them, at least one is bound to be available. You only need one! Some cities and towns have more than others. All it takes is a low assumption fee, some money down, and regardless of your credit history you can be a homeowner. Assumption fees are usually less than $150.

We purchased our home using the FHA assumable no-qualifying assumption technique. We knew there was no other way for us to qualify for a mortgage at normal interest rates only a few months after bankruptcy. This method is not for everyone. Let's look at the details.

ASSUMPTIONS VS. NO-QUALIFY ASSUMPTIONS

There is a difference between regular assumptions and no-qualify assumptions. Assumptions require credit approval. This means you will need to prove your creditworthiness in order to obtain financing.

No-qualify assumptions are as the name implies: No qualification is necessary to mortgage the home. No verification of income. No tax returns. No credit check. Nothing. In fact, on the day we became first-time homeowners my bankruptcy wasn't even discharged yet!

Literally anyone can become a homeowner in the United States today by using the FHA assumable no-qualifying mortgage technique. You don't even need a job. In fact, someone just out of jail could own a home through a no-qualify assumption.

WHY IS A MORTGAGE IMPORTANT?

A mortgage is a good idea for many reasons. Although everyone will have their own reasons for wanting a mortgage, here are some of the reasons that motivated us to become homeowners.

1.   A mortgage payment can be cheaper than rent.

2.   Mortgage interest is usually tax-deductible.

3.   The opportunity to build equity as the home appreciates.

4.   Stability. Home ownership gives you stability in the eyes of lenders.

5.   Pride of ownership. It's a good feeling that some day you will actually own the home. You are no longer a renter.

6.   Having a mortgage greatly improves your chances of qualifying for more credit.

7.   Some companies automatically extend you credit for merely being a homeowner.

HOW TO FIND NO-QUALIFY ASSUMPTIONS

You have two choices in locating FHA assumable no-qualifying assumptions: use an experienced Realtor who specializes in creative financing, or do it yourself.

We elected to work with a Realtor. The best way to find a creative Realtor is look at their ads in the black-and-white homes magazines. We looked for any hint that the Realtor was experienced in creative financing. Words like "creative financing," "owner-financing," "land contract," "assumption," and "no-qualify." These are good clues.

We also found several creative Realtors in the Sunday classifieds. We found our creative Realtors under the heading "creative financing." We called a few of them and asked a lot of questions. Both Realtors found us properties.

HOW TO INTERVIEW A REALTOR

It's important to find the right Realtor. Most of them do not understand FHA assumable no-qualifying mortgages, nor do they want to work with people who need them. This makes no sense. This is simple ignorance on their part. Sort of like hating another human being because of the color of their skin. Ignorance personified.

Work with an experienced Realtor who understands or specializes in creative financing. Take the time to find the right Realtor. It makes the whole process so much easier, and more enjoyable.

Realtors offer a big advantage. It's called the Multiple Listing Service, or MLS. An MLS is a local database of information on all the homes currently available for sale through Realtors. Over 97% of all properties for sale are listed with Realtors. The only homes you will not have access to through the MLS are the for-sale-by-owners.

At their MLS computer terminal they can type a request such as: "Show me all the FHA assumable no-qualifying mortgages on the northeast side of town that have at least two bedrooms, two baths, with a garage." Their MLS computer within seconds will tell the Realtor what is available. In less than 10 minutes the results will be printed, with pictures.

Some cities have more than one MLS. In this case it's important to decide where you would like to live before you begin looking for a Realtor. It's best to work with a Realtor who knows a particular geographical area. Interview Realtors one at a time until you find one who understands your needs, has experience in FHA assumable no-qualifying mortgages, has a positive attitude, knows the area you desire to move into, and enjoys working with home buyers. Remember, a Realtor gets paid only when he or she sells you a house. So if they feel you're wasting their time, you won't keep their attention.

Some small towns do not have an MLS. For towns like this, I would recommend that you consider *moving*. Really. It's usually very difficult to find no-qualifying assumptions in small towns without an MLS. The exception would be to find the Realtor who has been in the business the longest. These people are usually current or past presidents of the Board of Realtors. The Board of Realtors is the organization that all Realtors belong to. They are the ones that provide the MLS to the Realtors and maintain the data. Call the Board of Realtors and ask for the name and telephone number of the current president of the board. Ask this person for help in finding an FHA assumable no-qualifying mortgage. Otherwise, *move*.

I was born and raised in a small town. Recently I helped my mother look for a new home. I asked a few experienced Realtors about no-qualifying mortgages and was told "...not to waste my time, since there are none..." This small town had a simple MLS, but their MLS software did not allow them to search on homes with an assumable mortgage. This particular Realtor did not want to take the extra time to help find them. Do not work with Realtors like this.

Incidentally, the opportunity to mortgage a home was the major reason we moved from South Bend to Indianapolis. You simply have much more opportunity in larger cities. In addition, Realtors seem more knowledgeable on no-qualifying mortgages in larger cities.

Before you move, be sure the area you're moving to has a plentiful supply of FHA assumption no-qualifying mortgages. Call the Chamber of Commerce and request a "relocation kit." Ask them how to get a copy of the most recent black-and-white and/or color homes magazines. Purchase a copy of the Sunday newspaper and look through the real estate classifieds for creative Realtors. Most of the good ones offer toll-free numbers. If they don't, it could be an indication that they are not customer-driven. Ask a lot of questions. If this all seems like a lot of work, call the After Bankruptcy Foundation at (317) 578-7118 and inquire about their free Realtor referral service.

Another nice feature about MLS's is the "prospect feature." This feature will allow your Realtor to plug in what kind of home you're looking for, so when new listings post to the computer it will automatically notify the Realtor that there is a possible match that meets your requirements. In this case, a no-qualifying mortgage in a certain price range or in a particular part of town.

Since there are several different MLS software packages available on the market, each software vendor calls this feature something different. But you get the idea. Ask whether your Realtor can do this for you.

So now that you know enough to be dangerous, what questions are necessary to ask a Realtor to determine whether they are the one for you?

1.   Do you have experience in working with FHA assumable no-qualifying mortgages?

2.   Are you interested in helping me find one within the next 30 days?

3.   When was the last time you closed a deal like this?

4.   Is it possible to find a no-qualifying mortgage in this area of town?

4.   If not, where should I be looking?

5.   What would you do if you were me?

Their attitude is very important here. If they tell you "Don't get your hopes up" or "I hope you have a lot of money to put down"—this Realtor is not for you. You want a Realtor with an attitude of "one way or another we will get you a mortgage."

Notice that I didn't say *house*, I said *mortgage*. It makes all the difference in the world to obtain a mortgage. Without a mortgage you are still a renter.

DOES THE REALTOR NEED TO KNOW THAT YOU FILED BANKRUPTCY?

I would not volunteer this information immediately. You don't even know if you have the right Realtor yet. And besides, the Realtor won't decide if you get a loan or not. Their main concerns are: if you have money to put down and have a compelling reason to find a home—fast. The worst thing you can do to a Realtor is waste their time.

If the Realtor asks about your financial situation, tell the truth. Be prepared to back up the truth with a positive "sound bite." A sound bite is a memorized 15 to 30-second advertisement that comes out of your mouth to give someone encouragement that you're on the road to financial recovery.

The conversation might go something like this:

REALTOR: Why do you need to purchase a no-qualify assumption?

BUYER: We have a previous bankruptcy, and we don't
            believe we could qualify until we have at least
            24 months after discharge.
REALTOR: (Silence)
BUYER: However, we both started new jobs and have
            been working for six months. We have a new
            Visa bank card. Our bank approved us for a bank
            loan. We have $2,000 in savings. We just leased
            a new car. We have little debt, and no intention
            of spending more than we make again. We just
            need a second chance. Can you help us?
REALTOR: Why did you file bankruptcy?

Some of the best reasons you filed bankruptcy are: medical or loss of job due to layoff. Avoid the temptation to tell them your "long story," because they don't care. Focus on what is going on now. A 15-second sound bite would be good here.

At this point, if the Realtor feels that you're an honest person he or she will more than likely help you.

If a no-qualify assumption is a long shot in your area, your Realtor may be knowledgeable about first-time home buyer programs in your area. Or call the nearest housing authority listed in the Appendix.

QUESTIONS A REALTOR WILL ASK YOU

The more a good Realtor knows, the better. Remember how they are compensated. They do not get paid for their time. They receive income only when they sell homes. They have a right to be selective in whom they work with. If you just filed bankruptcy, have no money to put down and no way to save money any time soon—all good Realtors will say "goodbye" very quickly. You are not worth their time right now. Give them reasons to want to work with you.

They will ask a few questions, so be prepared with good answers. A good Realtor's line of questioning will go something like this:

1.   How much do you have available now for a down

payment on a house?

2. How much more money can you come up with in 60 days?

3. Why did you file bankruptcy?

4. How long ago was the bankruptcy discharged?

5. Where do you work?

6. What monthly payment can you afford?

7. Where do you live now, and how much do you pay?

8. When do you want to be a homeowner?

9. Have you re-established any credit since the bankruptcy?

How much money you have to put down gives them a better idea as to how serious you are about buying a home. We recommend having a minimum of $2,000 available, unless you're interested in a first-time homebuyer program. The more cash you have down, the more options you will have.

We had only $500 in our checking account when we found our house. We were confident we could save whatever was necessary within a short amount of time. It normally takes at least 30 days to close a mortgage. That's 30 more days of saving and doing everything we could to find the money.

Mentioning that you can come up with X more dollars in X days will also help. But don't stretch yourself too much. Be realistic. The Realtor will count on what you say.

The reason you filed bankruptcy is important. Certain reasons that can be verified, like medical or layoffs, sometimes allow the borrower to qualify for conventional or FHA financing earlier than usual. This is not the norm, however. Please spare the Realtor from hearing "your story"—they really don't care. Summarize the reason for your bankruptcy in one or two sentences and be done with it.

Realtors experienced in creative financing know current lending standards. They know it takes only 24 months of excellent payment history and re-established credit after a bankruptcy discharge to qualify for FHA or conventional financing. You may have more options than FHA no-qualifying mortgages.

When they ask you about your job, they are really probing to determine how much money you make and how long you've been employed. Know how much you gross each month. When asked, give a strong, confident answer. If your income will change drastically soon, be sure to share this information.

Know how much of a house payment you can afford. It's best to give your Realtor a price range, like $450 to $700 a month including taxes and insurance. It's best to stay at the lower end of the payment scale. The mortgage check is easier to write at the beginning of the month.

If they ask where you live, tell them. This may be a good indicator of how serious a buyer you are. If you've been in a small apartment for two years and you're ready to climb the walls, say so, in a nice way. This is good motivation. On the other side of the issue, if you're living with parents, the motivation may not be strong, unless you can convince your Realtor otherwise.

How much you are currently paying is a good indication of how much rent you can afford. If you're embarrassed because you are not paying rent, or your rent is low, simply say, "This allows us to save more money for our down payment each month." Realtors like to hear that.

Realtors are constantly probing you to determine your current level of motivation to buy a house. Remember, they get paid only when they sell one. If you've gone "cold," don't expect a lot of attention until you return to "hot" status. Realtors like spending time with "hot" prospects. If your attitude is "Whenever the right house comes on the market I will buy," you will not attention. Your attitude should be more like "We must be in a house within three months, at the very latest four months," or "We're ready to move as soon as possible." This is music to a good Realtor's ears. This shows motivation to become a home buyer.

Most Realtors will not ask whether you have re-established credit after bankruptcy. But it's important to share this with them. Remember, they don't care to know details. Just stick with the facts. And have an open mind; they may know of a better opportunity.

By your third or fourth Realtor interview you will know more about assumable mortgages than most Realtors do.

HIRING A REALTOR AS
A BUYER'S AGENT

Most Realtors work for the seller of the home. Within the last few years "buyer's agents" have become popular. Buyer's agents work for the buyer. They can share information with you that a traditional Realtor cannot. Whenever possible, work with a buyer's agent. It's as simple as asking whether they can represent you as a buyer's agent. Before you do this, be sure you found the right Realtor. Once you sign an agreement, you're done looking.

WORKING WITH NUMBER ONE REALTORS

Another option is to find a Realtor who will loan you part of their commission, or delay the commission to close the deal. This happens a lot with the top Realtors who are production-driven, especially at the end of the month or near the end of the year. The top Realtors who earn $500,000 or more a year can afford to delay the commission or do creative things, since they're constantly selling houses.

So how do you find the top Realtors? Look at Realtor ads in homes magazines, probably the color homes magazines if you have one in your area. Realtors like to announce that they are the number one agent in their ads. Read the ads. Another way is to pay attention to whose "for sale" signs you see a lot of in high-priced areas. How many signs you see of one particular agent could be a sign in itself. Another good way is to ask Realtors over the telephone who is the number one Realtor in the area.

It's usually important to stick with the number one Realtor in a particular state. The difference between the number one and number two Realtor can mean a lot of money. In Indiana, the number one Realtor by volume, Randy Keys with ERA Realty Centre, did three times as much volume as the number two guy. That's a lot. He can afford to be creative, whereas the number two guy may not be able to.

That last sentence is important. The Realtor doesn't owe you anything. Helping you is completely at their own discretion. Make your first impression count.

One Realtor I know sometimes takes his commission in the form of material things. He can't afford to do that for every deal, but it is done. He's taken several cars instead of a commission. He even took fur coats and jewelry. Do you have something of value that someone might want? Or maybe a talent to barter with? Anything is possible, you just have to ask. And not only ask, but ask the right person.

Don't bother asking someone new in the business, because you won't get very far. Don't waste your time with people who are new to the business. You want a proven professional who has experience.

IT'S NOT A DEAL UNTIL AFTER INSPECTIONS

Another option is to not worry about the down payment until after the inspections are complete—focusing your attention on houses that need repair and finding a creative title company. A good example is how our friends Bob and Patty mortgaged their home.

Bob and Patty saved $2,000 to put down on a house. They found a house, but it was listed for $100,000. They made an offer of $85,000 with a $500 earnest-money deposit, and it was accepted. In the offer they requested that inspections be done on the property. The inspection reports came back a week later listing several major repairs that needed to be done. Instead of bringing $2,000 to closing, Bob and Patty were told to bring $800. The title company simply subtracted the needed repairs off the down payment. In addition, Bob and Patty received a check from the seller on the same day to cover additional repairs totaling $650. It only took $150 to get into the house. Anything is possible if you can believe.

17

Key Things About FHA No-Qualifying Assumption Mortgages

THERE ARE CERTAIN THINGS you must know before you can decide whether you are a no-qualifying assumption home buyer.

YOU'RE BUYING THE FINANCING

Most important is getting it through your head that you're buying the financing. If it weren't for the financing, you might not be buying a home right now. Forget your dream home for now. We liked to think of ours as a "short-term investment property."

We help friends buy homes all the time who have lists of "must-haves" for their new home. They must be in a certain area, must have a three-car garage, must have 4 bedrooms with a loft, must have contemporary interior, must be close to work, must be this and must be that. Forget it. You're buying the financing. After you've been in the house 24 months you can sell it at a profit (if you bought it right), and then buy your dream home. You need to re-establish credit first. The dream home comes later.

SEARCH PARAMETERS

The best search parameters you can give your Realtor are a general geographic area, like north, or northeast, and how many bedrooms. Beyond that, you may not be a no-qualify assumption buyer.

We knew we wanted to live on the north side of Indianapolis.

We preferred northeast, but were open to anything up north. Since it was just the two of us, a two bedroom would do. We also preferred a condo, since both of us were not into lawn maintenance.

BUY IN AN APPRECIATING AREA

Another service your Realtor can provide is comps. Comps, or comparables, compare your property with others like yours in the area.

Since we nicknamed our home a "short-term investment property," it was easier to be more logical about the purchase. The emotion was tamed. We were more excited about being able to actually have a mortgage.

The comps will quickly tell you whether the home you are considering is priced right. Not only are you looking for a no-qualify assumption, but if possible, looking for one that you can pick up inexpensively.

Ask for the statistics on how long a property takes to sell in that particular area. This is a good indication of value as well. It's common for homes in "hot" areas to sell in less than 30 days.

We figured our prospective home was undervalued by at least $20,000. The previous owner had moved before this property was sold and he was making two mortgage payments. He just wanted out. The home had 91 showings on the property, but no one had bought. The Realtor said a lot of the comments from people were that it was small and dark.

Less than a year later, after putting new white carpet in the place and painting the wood and walls white, the house appraised for over $30,000 more than we paid for it. Now that's appreciation. If you buy smart, you will have more options down the road.

AVOID THE MOST EXPENSIVE HOUSE

Never purchase the most expensive house in the area. And also never purchase the most *inexpensive* house in the area. You will receive more appreciation in a shorter amount of time by being in the middle.

When you go to sell you will have a much easier time than the person who has the most expensive house. This person will usually lose money.

LOOK FOR HOMES THAT NEED MINOR
TENDER LOVING CARE (TLC)

When my wife took me to preview the home that later ended up to be our home, I wouldn't even go in. It was "beneath me." The carpet was ugly brown. The walls were dark. And there was a lot of wood.

This house needed some TLC. A lot of houses that offer no-qualify assumptions will need some work. Remember, these are homes built before December 1986.

Homes that need minor TLC represent the best possible chance for high appreciation. I am not talking about tearing out walls and adding onto the existing structure. More like new carpet, new paint, new countertops, remove wallpaper, etc.

Expect homes that need TLC.

IN A HURRY?

Don't be. Finding a simple assumption takes time. We began looking in early April, made an offer in late April, and became homeowners in early May. We moved in on the weekend most everyone in the world was watching the Indianapolis 500 in 1993.

The Realtor we used was experienced. She was good. Without her we would probably still be looking. Take the necessary time to find a good Realtor.

BE PREPARED FOR NEGATIVE PEOPLE

You will receive a lot of opinions about what is right and wrong for you to do, even from very capable Realtors. Attitude is everything, so be careful. Responses like "There just aren't many no-qualify assumptions out there" or "Maybe you should qualify for a normal mortgage" are indicators of a Realtor who doesn't have the right attitude. Smile, thank them for your time, and move on.

FIRST IMPRESSIONS ARE REMEMBERED

It helps to dress appropriately when meeting the Realtor for the first time. First impressions count. Be nice, positive, have a firm handshake, and smile a lot. If you're with a spouse, do not argue. Be on your best behavior. Remember, you are selling yourself to someone who will represent you.

MAKE IT EASY ON THE REALTOR

The Realtor will need to put a little more effort into helping you find a home than he or she would with a normal buyer. So have the attitude of doing whatever it takes to save him or her time. One of the best things you can do is offer to do "drive-bys." Drive by the home to see if it's something you would consider. Showing homes takes time. The more homes you see, the more time the Realtor has invested. Time is money to a Realtor. Offer to do as much legwork as possible. Not only will you establish a better relationship with your Realtor, but you will increase your odds of finding something faster.

HOW MUCH SECURITY DEPOSIT IS NECESSARY?

In Indiana, it is common to put down $500 to $1,000 with your offer as your earnest-money deposit. Put down as little as possible. Your money isn't earning any interest.

This will vary from city to city. Be sure to have a clause in your offer that if you are unable to obtain financing, your earnest money will be returned to you.

Five hundred dollars is all we had in our checking account the day we made our offer to purchase our home. We had less than 30 days to come up with the balance.

It's interesting—I never would have thought it was possible to save $2,000 in less than 30 days, but we did it. Well, actually we were $1,500 short on the day of closing. We worked out a deal with the Realtor who sold us the property that $100 a week would be directly taken out of my wife's check until it was paid in full.

Anything is possible when you can see the reward.

TOTAL CASH NEEDED

The one challenge with no-qualify assumption mortgages is the amount of equity in the home when the original owner wants to sell. This translates into how much cash the owner needs at closing.

It's common for the owner of a no-qualify assumption mortgage to have $5,000 to $20,000 of equity in the home. How they convert that into cash is by selling their home outright to someone who can put a new mortgage on it, thus paying off the existing mortgage and cashing them out.

Although I would recommend searching for no-qualify assumptions with low equity (just another search parameter on the MLS computer), do not be discouraged by high equity. Anything is possible. It depends on the owner's needs.

The owner may take a much lower price for the property than what it's currently listed at. This is one of the quickest ways to reduce the amount of equity perceived to be in the property.

In addition, there may need to be some important work to bring the house into livable condition. You can take this off the sale price as well.

The Realtor may be willing to let you borrow a portion of the commission, or delay the commission for a period of time.

And don't forget about owner financing. The owner may be in a position to "loan you the money" in the form of a second mortgage or even a side note. If he or she needs to sell it fast, it may be an option. This is one area where an experienced Realtor can negotiate on your behalf to help the homeowner see the benefits of giving you a second mortgage. However, if the owner needs to sell his or her existing house to qualify for a mortgage on their next house, the chances are bleak. Every situation is different. You find out by asking.

For more on creative financing, purchase Carleton Sheets' No Down Payment course. It doesn't get any better. You may contact his office at (800) 438-5553.

BE IN AGREEMENT WITH YOUR WIFE

Those of you who are married men, listen to your wife. There is power in agreement.

My wife and I made a promise to be in agreement on the purchase of our home, no matter what. As we began our home search, we quickly learned that we had different ideas on what we wanted in a house. The house I wanted (the first one we saw), she "didn't get a good feel about."

It took me a while to realize that women are born with this natural instinct to "feel" things. It's kind of like a sixth sense. Women are born with it, but men can learn it.

As it turned out, the house she thought we should buy was the one we ended up with. I hated it. It wasn't the palace I had envisioned, but it quickly became one. It appraised less than one year later for over $30,000 more than we paid for it. I have now learned to listen more to my wife.

We each brought important strengths into the agreement. I had faith that we could find a house and get a mortgage. She understood the local real estate market. We complemented each other. Look for each other's strengths.

WHAT TO EXPECT AT CLOSING

Closing is a term used in the real estate business that means the day the ownership is transferred. This happens once the appropriate documents are signed and certified funds are received.

The closing should be simply an exciting time where you sign legal documents. All your questions should be answered before the closing date.

A few days before the closing is scheduled, your Realtor should inform you of the exact amount in certified funds to bring to closing. Realtors normally do not know this exact figure until sometimes hours, but preferably days, before the closing. They rely on the title company to run the numbers.

Any problems with the title work, ownership issues, legal problems, tax lien issues, etc., should be discovered weeks before you are scheduled to close. Especially with an FHA assumable no-qualifying mortgage.

No-qualifying assumptions are easier to close compared with traditional mortgages. There is far less paperwork involved, so ask for a discount on your title work.

In Indiana you usually meet at a title company in a small room with your Realtor and a representative from the title company who has prepared your paperwork.

The title-company representative briefly describes what you're going to sign, then you sign where appropriate. The whole thing can take less than 45 minutes, depending on how many questions you have. Once you have finished signing all the documents, you provide the certified funds and the house is yours.

If you're one of those persons who need to read every line of legal jargon you sign, even though they are standard forms, tell your Realtor this in advance. If you don't, you may not close on that day.

Title companies have numerous "closings" scheduled throughout the day, and your Realtor has other homes to sell. Holding up the closing because you need to read everything is rude. It may result in the closing being rescheduled to another day, perhaps weeks away.

Your Realtor will gladly ask the title company to prepare a copy of the paperwork for your review before the closing date. You only need to ask.

My friend David was one of those people. He insisted that he read every document word for word before signing. His Realtor sensed that he was going to be difficult, and suggested reviewing the documents at the title company the day before the closing. So everyone was happy.

When I asked him whether he understood anything he read, he quietly replied, "No." It just made him feel better. This brings up a good point. It may be a good idea to engage the services of an attorney at a different title company to review the documents for you. Although I do not feel this is necessary, it may give you peace of mind. Ask your Realtor for a referral.

Most people don't realize all the services a title company can offer. In fact, all the paperwork in a mortgage transaction can be done at a title company. They even have attorneys on staff to review documents.

Another Realtor friend says new lawyers are always the ones who delay closing. They feel they have something to prove to everyone. If you're a new attorney, ask to review the documents before closing. Be considerate of other people's time.

Another important thing to remember about closing is that the title company will accept only certified funds. Both buyer and seller need to present certified funds at closing.

A lot of people assume that certified funds means anything a bank will provide. This is not the case. Money orders may not be considered certified funds in your area. Ask your title company what qualifies as certified funds to be presented at closing. Avoid a last-minute dash to the bank.

Our closing was close to a disaster. We were short of cash. I received the check we were expecting to allow us to close, but the bank put a seven-day hold on it, since it was for a large amount of money and it was out-of-state. Keep these things in mind before your closing date.

We simply told our Realtor what happened. She made the decision to proceed with the closing. The deal was that she was going to lend us what we needed, to be paid back weekly until paid in full. We were short about $1,200. This was less than her commission, so it was easy for her to do.

We were lucky that our Realtor was able to do that. If we had an new Realtor it never would have happened, and we probably wouldn't have become homeowners so fast.

Does this mean that every Realtor will want to lend you their commission? Certainly not. They must live too! But it helps if you work with someone who can help. Keep this as a last resort.

AFTER CLOSING

Three weeks after the closing, call your new mortgage company and ask a few questions:

1. When is my payment due?
2. When is the latest date I can pay before I am assessed a late fee?
3. Where or how else can I make a payment?

4.   How long does a payment take to post?
5.   Do you have a different mailing address to receive overnight payments?
6.   Which credit bureaus do you report to? How often?

You may preface a few of these questions with "Although I plan to always pay early or on time, it is good to know in an emergency."

We have never had the misfortune of being late on any revolving debt reported to the credit reporting agencies since the bankruptcy. My wife manages our accounts, keeps them up to date, and sends the payments on a timely basis.

Decide whose responsibility it will be to make sure the mortgage payment will be paid early or on time each month. Better yet, consider having your mortgage company automatically debit the mortgage payment from your checking account on a certain day each month. Although this may work for some people, I feel more comfortable in having the flexibility to pay when I want to.

Only after calling our mortgage company did we find out that we could make payments at a few bank branches they owned. We didn't know they were affiliated with the bank. This became very convenient in the early days. We could wait until the very last day before it was considered late to make the mortgage payment, in case we were short that month.

We learned that it took two days for the payment to post to our account. So we adjusted our payment schedule accordingly. Remember—early or on time!

Ask a lot of questions, even if you feel you know the answers. You will always learn something you did not know before.

CREATE A MORTGAGE FOLDER

You will refer to the closing documents from time to time. Create a mortgage folder and put it in a safe place. *Make it a policy never to allow anyone to use the originals; only give copies of what is needed.*

18

Understanding the Mortgage Players

BEING APPROVED FOR A mortgage after bankruptcy is easier than receiving overdraft protection on your checking account. The key is to understand where to shop your deal.

There are banks, mortgage companies that specialize in mortgage lending, mortgage brokers, credit unions, finance companies, captive mortgage companies, and nonprofit organizations. To make matters more confusing, some lenders handle nothing but conventional financing, others do FHA and VA financing. Then there are sub-prime lenders, and finance companies. Let's compare the benefits of a few of them.

BANKS

Banks may be a good source of financing if you have two years after discharge and outstanding credit since the bankruptcy. A bank reference is one of the best references to have on your credit reports. Another benefit to bank financing is that the loan usually costs less in up front fees. Each bank has its own policy regarding how it handles people with previous bankrupticies. So the first item of business is to determine which ones will help you if you've had a previous bankruptcy.

Banks have strict lending guidelines. Not all banks are created equal. Whom they sell their mortgages to depends on whether they can get you financing. Stay away from banks that sell their mortgages to Freddie Mac. Freddie's guidelines are too strict. Focus on banks that sell their mortgages to Fannie Mae or FHA. You just need to find the right bank.

Our Realtor referred us to a local bank in Indianapolis. Ask your Realtor for recommendations. A good Realtor closes a deal often, sometimes every other day. They know which banks are financing your type of deal.

Realtors will be reluctant to give away their contacts to just anyone who calls. Their livelihood depends on contacts. Make sure you have a relationship set up with your Realtor. If not, you'll have a lot of telephoning to do on your own to find the right mortgage lender.

And just because a lender cannot help you now, it may in the future. Lending requirements change constantly, and new programs are being developed every week. Keep calling back and ask whether anything has changed. You will be surprised. The idea is to get the lender to remember you so that when a new program does become available the lender will remember to call you.

MORTGAGE COMPANIES

The size of a mortgage company makes no difference. It's the person handling your loan that counts. You're looking for someone who understands your needs and will go the extra mile for you. These people are out there, and relatively easy to find. The best place to locate a good mortgage company is to call all the mortgage companies listed in the Yellow Pages. Look for multiple locations, big ads, medium-size ads, or number of years in business. Pay attention to the little things like how quickly they answer the telephone.

It's important to pick the right mortgage company for your deal. A lot depends on your individual situation:

- How long your bankruptcy has been discharged
- How you've paid your bills since the bankruptcy
- What new credit you've established since the bankruptcy
- How much money you can put down

Every mortgage company seems to have a specialty these days. If you don't have a lot of money to put down, you need to contact an FHA lender or inquire about a first-time home buyer program. If you have two years after discharge, you could go conventional if you have 3% to 5% to put down. Then there's the sub-prime lenders, also known as B,C, D or alternative lenders. These companies can put you into a mortgage at a slightly higher interest rate if you don't currently meet the conventional lending guidelines. The best sub-prime companies will refinance your mortgage into a conventional rate once you meet the guidelines.

Sub-prime lenders have a slight advantage, since their loans are not completely controlled by your credit score, unlike conventional lenders. Sub-prime lenders take a look at the complete picture. The trade-off is a slightly higher interest rate.

Then there are lenders that do nothing but equity-based loans for current homeowners. And the list goes on. The best thing to do is ask a lot of questions.

MORTGAGE BROKERS

This group is usually highly motivated to help you. It's also the most expensive option. They get paid well for taking the extra time to work difficult loans in the form of upfront and back-end fees.

The good thing about mortgage brokers is that they have many more funding sources available to them. Where a bank or mortgage company may only have a few resources, mortgage brokers have 20, 40, sometimes more than 60 different lenders they can sell your deal through.

It's important to contact several mortgage brokers. As with anything else, there are few good ones and many bad ones.

CREDIT UNIONS

As long as the credit union reports to all three credit reporting agencies, this could be a good alternative. If they do not report to all three credit bureaus, walk away. Most credit unions do not report.

QUESTIONS TO ASK

1.   Ask their policy on extending credit to people with a previous bankruptcy.

2.   If they cannot help you, be sure to ask, "If you were me what would you do?" or "Is there anyone you can recommend who may be able to help me?" Do not overlook the simplicity of these two questions. They are what lead us to the majority of our success.

Some companies will come right out and say they don't loan money to people who have filed bankruptcy. No matter. Don't get discouraged. There are other fish in the sea.

If you find a company that shows promise, simply:

1.   Tell them what you need.

2.   Give them a 30-second sound bite on what you have accomplished since your bankruptcy. Spare telling them your story, unless they ask. (they won't).

3.   Ask them if it sounds like they can help you.

4.   Ask them to describe a few tough deals they have been able to get done recently, specifically any with a previous bankruptcy.

5.   Ask whether they will review a recent credit report to avoid an inquiry until you feel more comfortable that they can get your deal done.

6.   Do not give your Social Security number or permission to pull a credit report until after they review your copy of your credit report.

7.   Ask what type of interest rate and terms go along with this type of deal.

8.   Be sure to tell them you have no interest in dealing with finance companies—only banks or reputable mortgage companies.

In preparing your sound bite, it should include:

1. When you filed bankruptcy
2. When your bankruptcy was discharged
3. What type of bankruptcy you filed
4. Which debt, if any, you reaffirmed
5. Any new credit you have re-established
6. Reason for bankruptcy, in one or two sentences
7. Length of employment
8. How much you earn each month
9. Debt-to-income ratio, if you have it
10. What type of income: W2 or 1099

A good sound bite should go something like this:

"We filed chapter 7 bankruptcy protection on February 1, 1993. It was discharged August 18, 1993. We reaffirmed with Sears and J.C. Penney's. Our current gross income is $45,000, and is 1099 income. We have been working for XYZ Company for 18 months. Since the bankruptcy we have mortgaged a new home with Waterfield, obtained a Visa bank card, leased two new cars through Ford. We save 10% of every paycheck in our bank account with Bank One. We filed bankruptcy because we simply spent more money than we earned, and have since have taken a whole new attitude, as our track record since the bankruptcy proves. Can you help me get a mortgage?"

Have fun calling. You'll meet a lot of interesting people who truly care about helping people. In the end, it will be obvious whom you should work with.

Half the battle is just determining which type of company to work with. And that decision rests with your individual situation. By talking with people and asking them what they think your options are, you will begin to see a pattern develop. Keep calling until you find a mortgage champion who really cares about getting your mortgage approved.

Start dialing now!

19

The "Best Buys" in Real Estate

YOU NEED TO KNOW where to find the "best buys" in real estate. I qualify a "best buy" as being a property that you can purchase at a price lower than what it's worth. Or, worst case, the ability for the property to appreciate quickly. There are five types of "best buys" to look for as you begin your search:

1. "Spec" homes
2. Old listings
3. Corporate owned listings
4. "Don't wanters"
5. Creative new-home builders

Why are these types of purchases considered the best buys? They hold the most promise for fast appreciation and the opportunity to purchase a home for less than appraised value.

OLD LISTINGS

Even though our mortgage was an FHA assumable no-qualifying mortgage, the home was on the market for a long time. The Realtor showed us 91 "showing slips." These are similar to telephone messages, but contain the response of the potential customers after they have seen the property. Ninety-one showings is a lot of showings. The average house is lucky to have 10 to 15 showings.

Our home had been on the market for over a year, and the owner was getting tired of making two house payments. And because of that we were in a really good position to negotiate the best price. In fact, the seller had to bring money to the closing. Usually the seller receives a check at closing.

It's important that you find out as much about the seller's situation as possible. If they need to sell their house before they move, chances are not as good, although possible. A better motivation for getting the best price is a divorce, two house payments, pending foreclosure, etc.

Find their motivation for selling. It's a good indication of what may be possible. Are you beginning to see why the Realtor is an important resource for you? A good one will find out as much as possible. Especially a buyer's agent.

By the way, if you really get a good price on a home, do yourself and your neighbors a favor and request a "confidential sale" from the MLS. Everyone will benefit long-term. This keeps the sale price and other details confidential.

"SPEC" HOMES

New home builders sometimes get caught in a pinch and need to sell a home they are building just to break even, because their spec home didn't sell as soon as expected. Why didn't it sell? Who knows. It could be anything from the color of the carpet to the number of bedrooms on the upper level. How do you find these homes? Most top Realtors know home builders that need to sell certain properties. All you need to do is tell them that what you're looking for. Our next home will be a builder's spec home.

CORPORATE-OWNED LISTINGS

Corporate-owned listings can be good buys. It depends on how long they have had it on their books. These properties originate from employees of large companies who were transferred. Part of the deal was that the company would be responsible for selling their home. Corporations do not like carrying homes on their books for very long. Good deals can be found here. Ask your Realtor to do a search on corporate-owned homes. Most Realtors who advertise anything to do with "relocation" can be more resourceful here than most Realtors who simply rely on the MLS data.

"DON'T WANTERS"

You or you Realtor won't usually know what is possible with a "don't wanter" until you make an offer. These home sellers know they are in a compromising situation, and usually don't tell their Realtor all the details until the last minute.

A good story about a "don't wanter" comes from our friends Bob and Patty. The house they wanted was listed at over $100,000. They told their Realtor to offer $85,000. A $15,000 discount off the top is unheard of in real estate, as a general rule. By law a Realtor must present all offers.

The owners accepted the offer. The house was weeks away from being foreclosed on. The previous owner had cancer and was dying. They just wanted out of the mortgage. The mortgage company just wanted what was owed on the mortgage. It became a win/win situation for everyone involved.

Now, I am not advocating that you go out and drag a Realtor around with you to make lowball offers all the time. It depends on the property. The property I mentioned supported a lower offer based on the comps in the area and the condition of the home.

Don't be afraid to offer low when the situation warrants. You just might find a "don't wanter."

CREATIVE NEW HOME BUILDERS

There's a growing trend developing where moderate-priced new-home builders assist home buyers in the financing with their own mortgage company.

These companies are worth a shot. Our friends Dean and Christine was recently approved for one. Sometimes you can do part of the work (like painting, laying carpet, etc.) to lower the amount of money you need to bring to closing. Some companies call them "sweat-equity" programs. The only way I know how to find them is by watching television commercials.

20

The Benefits of Being Pre-approved

THERE ARE MANY BENEFITS to being pre-approved for a mortgage. The biggest one is that you eliminate the chance of becoming greatly discouraged. Don't begin looking for a home until you speak with a mortgage professional first. The financing must be in place before you can even begin to look at homes.

Later, when you're re-established, you can purchase a home simply by finding the house first, then arranging the financing. But until then, you're buying the financing.

How do you find a creative mortgage lender that has a track record of getting difficult loans approved? Through your Realtor. When you find a Realtor you like, ask for a referral to a mortgage company that is experienced in difficult mortgages. If your Realtor does not have any contacts, move on. No contacts is a sign of inexperience. You don't have time to become someone's training ground.

Loan officers may also advertise in local black-and-white homes magazines. Look for key words in their ads that pertain to your situation. The bread and butter of their business is generated from Realtors. Realtors are constantly being wined and dined by mortgage companies to gain their business. Take advantage of these contacts. Ask, ask, ask.

Each mortgage company is different. You could get really discouraged on one phone call, and start dancing after finishing the second one. Just keep calling.

As long as you don't give out permission to pull a credit report, you're okay. Call as many mortgage lenders as you have time for. Get a feel for what is going on in your local market. Take good notes. Write down their name, the date, telephone numbers and comments from the conversation. If a particular person cannot help you, ask for a referral to someone who can. Or simply ask the question: "What would you do if you were me?"

Once you find a mortgage lender, ask them how to go about becoming pre-approved for a mortgage. If it's just a few minutes on the telephone, it's not a real pre-approval, it's a pre-qualification. There's a difference.

Being pre-qualified means absolutely nothing. It's a complete waste of time. You're looking to submit proof of income, tax returns, credit application, verify employment, and provide as much paperwork as possible. This is a real pre-approval.

Our friends Robert and Minna were tired of dealing with mortgage lenders that promised more than what they could deliver. They had given up on owning a home. They lost half of their earnest money due to the incompetence of an inexperienced Realtor.

They finally met a mortgage lender that got them pre-approved. Robert and Minna are in a really strong position now.

1.   They know exactly how much house they can afford.

2.   When making an offer, their Realtor can notify the seller that her buyers are pre-approved. This translates into a faster closing and a sure bet for the home seller. This is important when more than one offer is presented at the same time. Pre-approvals carry more weight.

3.   The stress and pressure has been relieved up front. Once they find the house, they can close within 2 to 3 weeks.

        Pre-approval is the way to go. Ask your mortgage lender about it. One of the advantages in attending our free Credit After Bankruptcy Seminar® is meeting local lenders. Call us; we will be glad to forward their names and telephone numbers to you.

21

Things That May Kill a Mortgage Application

ANTICIPATE A BUMPY RIDE until you walk out of the closing with the key to the home in your hand. This sounds negative, but it's best to be prepared.

People with a previous bankruptcy are in for a little ride. But hang in there. The twists and turns are well worth the hassle. Don't give up.

There are a few things to understand before making application for a mortgage. Understanding these items will prevent a lot of stress on yourself and your family.

There are things that will literally kill, or delay your chances of getting a mortgage. The potential mortgage deal killers are:

1. Unpaid tax liens or tax levies reporting on your credit reports
2. Poor credit since the bankruptcy
3. High debt-to-income ratio
4. Job instability
5. Hard-to-support income over last 24 months
6. Down payment
7. High expectations

UNPAID TAX LIENS OR LEVIES

Mortgage lenders do not lend to people with unpaid federal tax liens or levies unless they can be paid in full, or subordinated.

This is especially true with a refinance or home equity loan. On new purchases, if you have an installment agreement with the I.R.S. and at least a six month payment history, it's possible it won't affect your ability to get a new mortgage.

Subordinating debt to the IRS can and does happen when it's in the best interest of the IRS.

Your best bet to obtain a mortgage with unresolved tax problems is the FHA no-qualifying assumption mortgage, land contract or lease-purchase until the IRS situation is resolved or an installment agreement is in place.

My wife and I currently have an unpaid tax lien with the IRS. As of the date this was written, we anticipate to have it resolved by December 1998. At that time we intend to purchase a new home. A mortgage is important to us. We didn't want to become renters again, although the land-contract laws in Indiana allow several of the same tax benefits as having a mortgage. Re-establishing credit is our main objective right now.

POOR CREDIT SINCE BANKRUPTCY

Nothing will kill the deal quicker with conventional lenders than late payments on your credit report after a bankruptcy.

If you have accidentally been late on a payment, don't freak out yet. The first thing you need to do is request all three of your credit reports from your local credit reporting agencies to determine whether it has even been reported. If it's been 30 to 90 days since you were late and nothing shows, it may be safe to say that you're okay.

If something does show up, one of the first questions you must ask your mortgage lender is whether the late payment will prevent you from getting a loan. If you ignore handling this potential problem up front, you may be wasting everyone's time.

My wife and I had several state tax liens that showed up on our credit reports just before we closed on our home equity loan. We still received the home equity loan through a local bank, but it cost us more. I think the rate jumped an additional 1.5 points simply because there were unpaid state tax liens.

State tax liens don't seem to be as dreadful as federal tax liens with lenders in our area. Check with lenders in your area before you assume too much. You would be surprised at what they can ignore these days.

HIGH DEBT-TO-INCOME RATIO

The numbers will determine whether you can afford a mortgage or not. Unlike an FHA no-qualifying assumable mortgage, you must prove that you can afford the home you desire to purchase.

Mortgage lenders and banks use debt-to-income ratios. Ask them how they figure debt-to-income ratios for obtaining a mortgage. Don't worry about including small things like cable television, gasoline, grocery bills, etc. What they are concerned about is the regular monthly liabilities that report to your credit reports. (i.e., rent, association fees, car payments, bank card payments, department store cards, other loans, etc.)

If your debt-to-income ratio is high, ask their advice on ways to bring it down. It may include paying a few things off or even canceling some unnecessary credit cards. Show a sincere interest to make it happen, and mortgage lenders will work with you.

JOB INSTABILITY

Conventional mortgage lenders like to see you in the same line of work for at least 24 months before they will consider you stable. FHA lenders need only six months. You could have worked for four different firms during that time, but the key is that you're in the same line of work.

An important element in getting a mortgage is staying put until you close on your mortgage. After you close, you are free to try something new. A lot of people do this.

HARD-TO-SUPPORT INCOME

If your income has changed drastically in the last year, it will be difficult to meet lender guidelines. Typically, they look at the last two years based on your tax returns.

This means that if you had a bad year last year and made only $9,000, then turned around and made over $60,000 this year, even though your income supports it now you will have challenges in qualifying for a mortgage using traditional methods.

Your only hope at this point is to find a qualified mortgage professional who is more creative than the average lender. These people know how to provide the right documentation to get the deal done. They are out there; just start looking.

DOWN PAYMENT

There are numerous housing programs available to help people with their down payment. While FHA financing requires only a 3% down payment, conventional financing needs 3% to 5% down for most conforming mortgages.

First-time home buyer programs are unique in each community. If you don't have 3% to 5% to put down on a home, you'll need help in raising a down payment. The best way to find out about these programs is to:

1. Start with the Appendix in the back of this book.

2. Talk to Realtors.

3. Call the major banks in your area and ask whether they have any first-time home buyer programs or other creative ways to mortgage a home.

Be sure to always ask for a referral. Think of it as a treasure hunt and have fun. And don't stop looking once you find your first resource. Look at all of them, weigh your options, and go with the program best suited to your needs.

HIGH EXPECTATIONS

If you're like me, reality sometimes hurts. When we determined how much house payment we could afford and then looked at homes in that price range, I was shocked. My first reaction was, could people really live there?

I had high expectations, and this thinking initially got in my way. Remember, you're starting over. The dream home will come in time, but for now you need to prove yourself. The lower your payment, the better. The checks are easier to write.

22

How to Refinance Your Existing Mortgage

THE BEST PLACE TO start your search to refinance your existing mortgage is with your current mortgage company.

If you have an FHA mortgage, the government has provided another program that enables anyone to refinance their mortgage, regardless of credit history. It's called the FHA Streamline.

Here's how it works. You call a mortgage lender that offers an FHA Streamline program. They take a regular loan application and run a credit check. The only thing they look at is whether the mortgage payment has ever been late. If it hasn't, you qualify without having to prove income. In fact, in most cases a new appraisal is not even required.

We knew about the FHA Streamline before we purchased our first home. Our strategy was to mortgage our present home at 10.5% interest, then FHA Streamline it to 6% in six months after we closed. And we did just that.

FHA guidelines stipulate that you must wait at least six months before you can refinance. During that six months we interviewed several lenders. Everyone had a different type of program. In the end, we called the existing mortgage company and asked what kind of program they had. Their program beat all others hands down.

The most difficult thing for us was to prepay the first month's payment at closing. In essence, this meant we had to make two mortgage payments in one month! We did it. Each of us lost several pounds as we saved money from our food budget, held our first garage sale, and sold other things around the house. It was worth it. Our house payment went from $661.50 to $441.32.

Within 45 days we had a lower house payment, a lower interest rate, and more cash in our pocket in month.

When you use the FHA Streamline you don't receive any of the equity in your home—just an adjusted interest rate, which translates into a lower mortgage payment. Our motive was clearly a lower house payment to increase our cash flow.

The only downside to an FHA Streamline loan for those who have an FHA assumable no-qualifying mortgage is that the assumable part of the mortgage does not transfer to the new owner when you sell. So if we intended to allow the next owner to assume the mortgage, this would create a stumbling block.

Since our home had so much equity in it now, we doubted it would be within the range of a FHA assumable home buyer. So we Streamlined our mortgage.

One of the nice things about the FHA Streamline is that we now have two positive credit references on our credit reports: the old mortgage when we assumed it, and now our new mortgage. The more positive references, the better!

Your mortgage does not have to be an FHA assumable mortgage to take advantage of the FHA Streamline refinance. Look for mortgage lenders in the Yellow Pages or the black-and-white homes magazines that have the word "streamline" in the ads. Call them and inquire as to the requirements for a Streamline loan in your situation. Or contact any mortgage lender that can do FHA financing. Always ask for an end-of-month closing date, you will have to come up with less money at closing.

Mortgage lenders are the funniest people. All of them want your Social Security number. They will do and say anything to get it from you. Don't give it to them until you have interviewed several lenders and called your existing mortgage company.

Out of all of the people I worked with in re-establishing credit, these people were the most unreliable. Of course, once you find the right one it makes all the difference in the world. But until then, expect to meet some interesting people.

One man took a credit application, worked with me over a period of a week or so, and promised to call me with an answer in a few days. I still have never heard from him.

QUESTIONS TO ASK AN FHA STREAMLINE LOAN OFFICER

There isn't much to know about interviewing these people, since it is very close to a no-qualifying loan. Most of the questions revolve around how they do business. Start with the following questions:

1. Do you offer FHA Streamline mortgages?
2. Have you closed any?
3. Tell me how the FHA Streamline works.
4. Will the closing date affect how much money I bring to closing? If so, when is the best closing date?
5. What are the current interest rates?
6. I am paying % now, how much would I save if I would Streamline now?
7. Do you need to pull credit reports?
8. What are the credit qualifications?
9. How long does it take from start to finish?
10. Do you sell the mortgage to another company or hold it yourself?
11. If you sell my mortgage, who will service it, and where would I make payments?
12. Does the loan have a grace period?
13. What credit reporting agencies does the mortgage company report to?

After you have finished asking these questions, if the person is in an authority position he or she may ask you whether you want a job. People are not used to dealing with people who know what they are talking about. That's the impression you give by asking questions, even if you don't know the answers.

Incidentally, I chose our original mortgage company to do our FHA Streamline, simply because they are a well-known name in the mortgage business and the total out-of-pocket expenses were lower than with the other companies.

23

How to Get Approved
for a Home Equity Loan

I HOPE YOU HAVE your seat belt on. If your goal is to obtain a home equity loan shortly after bankruptcy, you may be in for a ride if your discharge isn't two years old yet.

Out of all the new credit we re-established, obtaining a home equity loan was the toughest, most frustrating, and most time-consuming. It didn't help matters that we were both self-employed and our income was hard-to-support.

Can you expect to receive a home equity loan? Yes. But do not be in a hurry. It will come, but it may take time.

Part of the problem lies with how the system is set up. The people who make the loan decisions, the underwriters, have little or no contact with the customer. The customer's sole contact is with the mortgage sales representative. So what's the problem? The mortgage rep is simply the liaison between the two. Everything is based on what the underwriter says. Aggressive salespeople are quick to say "No problem" before clearing it with their underwriters.

This system provides for a lot of problems. For one, most mortgage salespeople do not understand underwriting guidelines. They make plenty of promises, and then cannot deliver.

I constantly got suckered into the spin these people gave me. In the end, two out of about 31 mortgage salespeople could deliver.

Learn from our mistakes. I was turned down 29 times for a home equity loan by companies specializing in hard-to-finance loans. I wanted to beat the system that said I needed to wait 24 months after bankruptcy before they would consider a home equity loan. In the end, I had to wait the 24 months to get the best rate.

If I had $1,000 for every mortgage lender who said "No problem," I would have retired to the Bahamas by now. Be careful with these people. Take your time to find a reliable one who understands what you're trying to accomplish and is willing to go the extra mile for you. When they say "No problem," ask them to put it in writing and get it signed by the owner of the company.

ENOUGH EQUITY

You must have enough equity in the house for the loan to make sense. If you have only $5,000 or $10,000 in equity in your home, chances are you may not qualify for a home equity loan.

This is why it's so important, when looking for a home, to pay attention to how fast homes appreciate in the area, and the comparable figures for similar property in the neighborhood. If you ignore this, it will take time before you see significant equity built up in your home. So you first must purchase the right home at the right price to even be able to consider a home equity loan.

How to figure whether you have enough equity in your home is pretty straight forward.

APPRAISED VALUE TIMES 80%
MINUS LOAN PAYOFF = LOAN

If your house is appraised for $95,000 and the lender's standard loan-to-value ratio is 80%, you would multiply the two and subtract your loan payoff ($58,000) from this amount to arrive at the total loan amount available.

The higher the loan to value ratio used by the lender, the higher your interest rate may be. The lender sees it as a greater risk and therefore charges a higher rate. Check around; there are plenty of companies, even banks, that offer 150% loan to value deals now.

TWO-YEAR RULE

In the mortgage business, 24 months of excellent credit history is necessary to qualify. Thirty-six months if you've had a foreclosure. It's the "golden rule" in the industry. You could fight it, and find someone who would do it earlier. However, it will probably cost you significantly more in interest, run the risk of unnecessary credit inquiries on your credit reports, and cause a lot of frustration from rejection. My advice is to wait. Around 23 months after your discharge date, begin getting serious. As early as 12 months if you elect to go with a sub-prime lender for a short period of time. In the meantime, keep your eyes and ears open for possible resources. Cut out ads, write down telephone numbers, ask for referrals, and most of all, save money!

DIFFERENT TYPES OF MORTGAGE LOANS

There are a lot of loan programs to choose from. We chose a home equity loan as a revolving line of credit. However, there are non-revolving home equity loans, new first mortgages, a second mortgage, and an assortment of other options. Be sure you know what you want and can articulate your motivation for wanting it. You may need an entirely different product than you realize. Ask what the difference is between the lenders' products, since everyone seems to have different names for similar products. In Indiana it may mean one thing, but something entirely different in California.

BENEFITS OF A HOME EQUITY LOAN

The big reason the home equity loan is so popular is that it is one of the last 100% tax deductions for the average homeowner. You used to be able to deduct bank card interest, but that was phased out several years ago. Home equity interest is completely deductible. This can save you a ton of money at tax time. I know—we've write off nearly $6,000 in interest each year from our home equity loan. That's $6,000 less I have to pay the IRS on April 15.

CONDOS VS. SINGLE-FAMILY HOMES

We purchased a condo. I am certain we could have closed a home equity loan deal within the first 12 to 18 months after bankruptcy if we had purchased a single-family home. Condos, however convenient, have different lending restrictions. Don't let this fact prevent you from purchasing a condo, but know in advance that it is a little more difficult to get a home equity loan on a condo.

Some reasons for this have to do with the home owner's association and how it formed the development. In certain parts of the country, as in Indiana, they do not allow above 80% loan-to-value as a general guideline.

I am unsure why this is. You should run through a few "what if" scenarios with your existing mortgage company to determine when you would be able to apply for a home equity loan if you're planning to purchase a condo. Call the customer service department and ask a few questions. Tell them that you heard home equity loans are more difficult with condos than single-family homes. This should start the conversation in the right direction.

24

How to Lease a New Car After Bankruptcy

GETTING APPROVED FOR A new car at low-interest rates is very easy. It can happen the very day you receive your discharge letter from the bankruptcy court. The problem with most people is that they think their only option is to purchase a used car at high interest rates from a high-interest company. That's not the case.

MAZDA MIATA STORY

I had my heart set on a used red Mazda Miata within months after bankruptcy. I test-drove that car for two weekends. It felt good driving it with the top down, wind in my hair, music playing, warm weather—I was hooked.

It wasn't meant to be. I found the car. I located the financing through a high-interest finance company. Still, no matter how hard I tried, the two could not be put together. Needless to say, I did not become the owner of the used red Mazda Miata. As I look back, it was the best thing that could have happened to me. It helped me see that I had more options.

EXPECTATIONS

If you truly want to re-establish credit after bankruptcy and quickly rid yourself of the stigma associated with bankruptcy, your expectations must be in order. Forget the Mercedes, Miata, BMW, Jeep Cherokee, Infinity, Toyota Camry, and any other fine cars. What you should expect is a brand-new car at a normal interest rate through a reputable dealer.

OUR FIRST CAR

After the failed Mazda Miata experience, all I wanted was a car to drive. I began calling car dealers to determine who could get me financed. Since I am not fond of car salespeople, I always asked for the new car lease manager. I figured that once I found someone who could get me financed, it wouldn't matter whether the salesman was an idiot.

I visited a lot of car dealerships, never test-driving anything. Getting the financing was more important than becoming hooked emotionally to a certain car. After randomly visiting several car dealerships it was apparent that we needed a new game plan. No one could get us financed.

Then one day, after being turned down by Toyota Motor Credit, we became desperate. We needed a car. Something with four wheels. The "wish list" was thrown out the window, and we decided we wanted a new car we could afford.

I asked the Toyota leasing manager what he would do if he were me. What he said changed everything.

He told us that Ford Motor Credit had the best financing program in the country and if anyone could get us financed, they could. The program was called the Red Carpet Leasing Program. He went on to say that Ford usually approves loans he turns down. We can't even come close to what they offer, he said.

I was silent. My wife and I turned to each other with facial expressions that looked like we just ate a sour lemon. A Ford? Made in America? Will it fall apart? They got a kick out of our line of questioning. We were dead serious. We had never owned a Ford.

Knowing that Ford was our last chance to obtain mainstream credit for a new car, we decided to talk with Ford. The Toyota dealership recommended the Ford dealership across the street. The next day, with recent credit report in hand, I visited the Ford dealership. I met the new-car lease manager, Bob Spalding. Not wasting any time, my first question to Bob was, "Can you finance people with a previous bankruptcy?" His reply was a confident "Tell me more." I then sat down and proceeded to give him a "sound bite" of my accomplishments since the bankruptcy.

Bob then asked me a series of questions to qualify me. The questions ranged from how long ago the bankruptcy was discharged to how much money I could put down. After he finished questioning me, he was convinced something could be done, but he would need to look at my credit report.

I then asked whether he would review a recent copy of my credit report, which I had with me. I explained that having a credit inquiry on my credit report hurts me if I am turned down, and that I was trying to avoid unnecessary credit inquiries. He agreed. He looked my credit report over and said, "I think we can help you."

When I met Bob we hit it off right away. Then something really interesting happened. As we began talking about the monthly payment, he told me he had also filed bankruptcy. I was excited, and I knew we would be driving soon. And it gets better. After Bob and I talked about a comfortable monthly payment range, he introduced me to a car salesman, Troy. As Troy and I began walking through the car lot, he told me he had also filed bankruptcy!

At this point I knew Ford could get my deal done. My reasons were that both Bob and Troy were driving Ford cars and had previous bankruptcies. They understood my needs.

Now the only thing I needed to do was pick out the car, right? Wrong. I asked Bob to tell me which car would be easiest for me to get financing for with Ford. The only choice I wanted was the color of the car.

Bob's first choice was the ugliest car I have ever seen. I took one look at it and quickly went back to Bob and asked whether I had any other options. His response was, "Sure, but it will increase your down payment by $500. Why don't you go take a look at it?"

Troy then showed me the car. It was a brand-new 1993 Ford Escort. I liked it. A long way from a convertible BMW or Cherokee Jeep, but it was cute. I kept thinking that the financing from Ford Motor Credit was more important than status. This would improve my credit report. To me it was a short-term sacrifice that would have long-term benefits. Don't get me wrong, it was a very humbling experience.

I asked Bob to run the numbers on that car. After visiting several buy-here-pay-here dealerships I knew that my worst-case scenario would be to have to come up with $2,000 to put down on a used car at 21% interest if Bob's numbers didn't work.

As Bob was running the numbers, I called my wife. As I told her the car's make and model, her response was, "What is an Escort?" I convinced her that it was cute and to give it a look later that night.

Bob and I finally sat down to discuss the numbers. The good news was that the lease payment for a two-year lease right now through Ford would be less than $94 a month. The bad news was, to lease that car I would need around $1,500. I paused. I knew I only had $500 at the time, but the capacity to save more over time.

I then became very bold. I said to Bob, "I have $500 I can put down on this car today. Do you have the authority to allow me to spread the balance over, say, 30 to 45 days?" His response surprised me. He said confidently, "I think we can work something out. Let's submit this to Ford and see what they say."

Since it was late in the evening, he suggested that it was too late to submit it to Ford that day. And with his day off the following day, he would be unable to submit it until after his day off. I agreed. I trusted my "champion" to present my case in the best way he saw fit. I would wait for Bob. I drove home and waited for him to call.

I found out later that I was working with the largest Ford leasing dealership in Indiana. They funnel a lot of deals to Ford, so they have more flexibility than smaller dealerships. For instance, they might submit a package of 100 deals to Ford for approval at one time. Of those 100 deals, 90 would be good deals, while the other 10 would be marginal. The dealership would submit it to Ford as a package. Take them all or nothing. It is to your advantage to work with the largest Ford leasing dealer in your area.

Bob called back a few days later. It was a done deal. Ford had bought it. All that needed to be done was to sign the paperwork and draw up some type of agreement to pay the balance of the down payment over time. Even though we didn't have a clue exactly where the money was going to come from, we were happy. We were approved from a mainstream lender!

Bob asked for two postdated checks from us, with instructions that they would not be deposited until we called to confirm that they were good. My wife and I visited the dealership and drove our new 1993 Ford Escort off the lot that same day. The car was financed by Ford Motor Credit at 2.9% interest. We made the two postdated checks good, and everything was great.

Does this mean that your Ford dealer will offer to hold postdated checks for you? I don't know. Most dealerships do not. If you have $1,000 to put down, you may not need to. In fact, some Ford dealers who can approve deals with as little as $500 down! Kirk Varga at Theodore Robins Ford in Costa Mesa, California is one of the most creative Ford dealers I know. He can put people in new cars with no money down. Every city is different. Every Ford dealer is different. It makes a difference which Ford dealer you go to.

Our only sacrifice in our new car was a radio. Adding a radio would have increased our down payment by another $500. So our first car after bankruptcy was without a radio.

A note of caution: Do not choose the Ford dealer closest to you. Call them all. Some sell only trucks. Some push purchasing. Others push leasing. Look them up in the Yellow Pages. Ask a lot of questions. After you talk with them all, decide which two Ford dealers you feel can get you financed. Then visit each dealership with a copy of your credit report. Decide which Ford dealer has your best interests in mind. Once you turn in a credit application with a Ford dealer, it's extremely hard to switch dealers if you're turned-down.

Who has the best financing for a person with a previous bankruptcy? No question, Ford Motor Credit.

HOW TO APPROACH YOUR FORD DEALER

1.   Call the dealership and request to speak with the new-car lease manager.

2.   Ask whether they can finance someone after bankruptcy.

3. Give the person your 15-second "sound bite."

4. Ask when was the last time they financed someone with a bankruptcy.

5. Ask what the down payment range would be on a deal like yours.

6. Ask whether the finance manager will review a copy of your credit report to determine your chances of being approved before making an application.

7. Make a decision as to whether it's worth your time to visit the dealership in person. Do not give out your social security number yet.

8. Visit the best two Ford dealerships.

9. Avoid salespeople until you're introduced to one.

10. Develop rapport with the lease manager.

11. Ask yourself "Can this person get me financed?"

12. Choose one Ford dealer, and fill out a credit application.

13. Avoid the bankruptcy question on the credit application.

14. Ask the new-car lease manager what you should do.

15. Ask what car is best to lease right now.

16. Ask about any rebates or soft-dollar credits.

17. Begin to look at cars.

QUESTIONS FORD MAY ASK YOU

1. Do you have a trade-in?

2.   How long since your bankruptcy was discharged?

3.   What new credit have you established since bankruptcy?

4.   Have your bills since the bankruptcy been paid early or on time.

5.   How much money can you put down now?

6.   Was Ford included in your bankruptcy?

7.   Have you ever owned a car financed by Ford? If so, did you have any late payments?

8.   What is your payment range?

9.   Why do you need this car?

10. Why did you file bankruptcy?

Take your time and answer their questions honestly. Don't waste your time telling them "your story," they don't care. Focus on what you have accomplished since your bankruptcy.

FORD'S POINT SCORING SYSTEM

Ford Motor Credit uses a point scoring system to determine whether you will be financed through Ford. The most important questions on the application are:

1.   Do you own or rent?

2.   Do you have a phone in your name?

3.   Checking and savings accounts?

4.   Local bank references?

5.   Time on job: years/months?

6. Have you ever filed bankruptcy?

7. Have you re-established credit after bankruptcy?

You receive a higher point score if you own a home versus renting. Although owning a home is not required, it will give you a better score than if you rent.

Having a phone in your own name shows stability and is an indicator of creditworthiness. My wife and I have several telephone lines. Some are in her name and others in my name, specifically for this reason.

Checking and savings accounts are important to underwriters. If you have only a checking account, it's pretty easy to determine that you spend whatever you earn. If you have a savings account, it shows you're concerned about saving for your future.

A local bank reference is important. Bank references are looked at favorably. Do whatever it takes to establish a banking relationship, even if it's more expensive.

The more time on the job you have, the better. Always round off on the high side. This is not a question to underestimate. It is prudent that you have at least six months of job history in the same line of work before approaching any credit lender. Of course, I hear stories all the time that break all the rules.

It's important that you re-establish credit after bankruptcy. At minimum, you need three new credit references with on-time payment history, reporting to the credit reporting agencies.

The only question I will suggest that you ignore is the "Have you ever filed bankruptcy?" question. The reason you should ignore it is that the computer will automatically decline your credit application. It's much better to ignore the question on the application, communicate your situation to the lease manager, and let him do his job. I had a problem with this initially. I thought I was being dishonest. I came to realize that I was being up-front with everyone involved. Everyone would know I filed bankruptcy. The difference is that the computer wouldn't know. I am okay with it now, and I recommend that you do the same.

SOURCES FOR CAR FINANCING

The bankrupt person has several choices in deciding where to purchase his or her next car. Just take a look at your Sunday newspaper. It's full of car dealerships marketing to people with poor credit, no credit, slow credit, and bankruptcies.

However, the sources that speak directly to you are most likely not looking out for your best interests. Buyer beware. Let's take a look at a few of your options:

1. Buy-here-pay-here car lots
2. General finance companies
3. High-interest finance companies working exclusively with car dealers
4. Car dealers advertising creative financing
5. Credit-union financing
6. Bank financing
7. General leasing companies
8. Car-manufacturer lease financing

BUY-HERE-PAY-HERE CAR LOTS

Avoid these companies at all costs. You will recognize them by their advertising and their ability to carry the financing. The first negative is that you're not re-establishing "mainstream" credit. Second, most of these companies do not report to the credit reporting agencies. And if they did, who wants to see TOM'S USED CAR LOT on your credit report?

It's credit references such as TOM'S USED CAR LOT that will attract more crappy credit. If you think of yourself as that type of buyer, credit lenders will also think of you as that type of customer.

Most of these companies sell late-model cars. I would much prefer a new car with a full warranty. I don't have a lot of time for unexpected repairs. Time is valuable to me.

The good thing these companies provide is hope. It's a good feeling, as you're working at getting approved by a mainstream lender, that your worst-case scenario is one of these places if all else fails.

GENERAL FINANCE COMPANIES

The problem with using this type of financing is that it's not mainstream credit. Who in their right mind should pay 21% to 36% interest on a car loan?

Finance companies are considered the loan sharks of the lending business. Finance-company credit references do not give you the power position in re-establishing credit after bankruptcy. They weaken your case substantially. Stay away from them, and do not be enticed with their direct-mail solicitations.

HIGH-INTEREST CAR FINANCE COMPANIES

These finance companies have specific loan programs targeted toward car dealers. Car dealers like to give their customers options. So when you enter the showroom and do not meet normal lending criteria, they automatically submit your application to one of their high-interest finance company loan sources.

The names of these companies are designed to sound large and important. It's very misleading. Like general finance companies, they charge a premium interest rate, require a substantial down payment and/or security deposit, lend on late-model cars, and are not considered mainstream credit references on your credit report.

CAR DEALERS ADVERTISING CREATIVE FINANCING

There was a car dealership in Indianapolis that worked a deal with a large local bank to finance late-model cars. After noticing their ads in the Sunday newspaper, I called and asked a lot of questions.

Usually these car dealers belong to a program sponsored by a finance company at extremely high interest rates. However, there are a few good programs out there. The one in Indianapolis was a good bank-financed program. Bank financing is the next best thing to Ford Motor Credit. The only way to know is to call and ask the right questions.

1. You need to determine what type of company is providing the financing.
2. Is it a bank, "banc," finance, or lease financing?
3. If bank financing, which bank?
4. What are the terms?
5. How does the program work?
6. What are their credit requirements?
7. What down payment is necessary?
8. What is the average term of the loan?
9. Whom do I make my payments to?
10. What interest rate might a person with a previous bankruptcy expect to pay?
11. Who's name shows on your credit report?

If the financing is not provided by a bank, keep looking. This financing is not mainstream. No matter what gimmicks they use, it is not worth your time. Recently I opened up the automotive classified section and was surprised to see a few car dealerships offering a Visa bank card to anyone who purchased a car through them. As I read the fine print, it was easy to tell that this card was provided by the finance company that extended the financing. Don't be fooled by these gimmicks. This is not mainstream credit.

CREDIT-UNION FINANCING

Credit unions have one major flaw: They usually do not report to the credit reporting agencies. If your timely payments are not reported, you're spinning your wheels.

There are several very large credit unions around the country. Some are even bigger than banks in their area. If your credit union reports to the three major credit reporting agencies, they pass the first test. The second test is to determine how willing they are to help you re-establish credit after bankruptcy. Do they offer secured loans? Will you automatically receive a Visa debit card? When should you try to apply for overdraft protection? Can you print your new checks beginning with a high check number? When was the last time they helped someone with a previous bankruptcy? Ask questions.

BANK FINANCING

This is one of the best types of mainstream credit. There are few things more powerful than bank references on your credit report. The challenge is that most banks have a policy about extending credit to people who have previously filed bankruptcy. As a rule, they don't like us.

This is changing, but very slowly. The aggressive banks have special programs with local car dealerships. Bank financing may be a better option for someone who has several years of established credit after bankruptcy. For the new bankruptcy filer, bank financing is highly unlikely.

In my personal experience, I think that trying to get a car loan with a bank after bankruptcy is a waste of time. The exception to the rule is if they have created a special program with a car dealership. So, it's easy to see why a credit union could be tempting.

Don't give up on banks. Once you find the right bank manager, he or she is worth their weight in gold. It's finding creative bankers that is the challenging part.

GENERAL LEASING COMPANIES

Like banks, it is highly unlikely the new bankruptcy filer will qualify for general lease financing. However, I have heard stories of people receiving lease financing for cars using general leasing companies. This type of financing is typically reserved for people with a more established credit history.

Give yourself time, and eventually you will be able to qualify for this type of financing.

CAR-MANUFACTURER LEASE FINANCING

This is the ideal type of financing for anyone with a previous bankruptcy. Captive leasing companies, like Ford Motor Credit, have two reasons to get you into a car: (1) to sell you a car, and (2) to make money on the lease financing. Other types of financing earn money only by making the loan.

Ford Motor Credit takes less risk by extending a two-year

lease, compared to the typical five-year financing. Taking less risk means they can accept more risk. Don't be afraid of leasing. There are a lot of positives to leasing. A few are:

1. Easier to qualify with previous bankruptcy
2. Lower down payment
3. Lower payment than a purchase
4. At the end of the lease term you may either walk away, trade, purchase, or refinance
5. Shorter payment term
6. Possibly 100% tax-deductible (see your accountant)

The absolute best place to obtain financing on a brand-new car is Ford Motor Credit's Red Carpet Lease program.

Purchase financing can also be done through Ford Motor Credit. Some friends of ours, David and Tammy, needed a car and purchased a used car through Ford. They still received the Ford credit reference, but because of their extremely low income they could not qualify for a new-car lease. The important thing is the mainstream credit you're establishing by working with Ford Motor Credit.

The big picture is even better. Once you establish yourself with Ford Motor Credit and you pay them as agreed, you can virtually finance your next car in minutes.

OUR SECOND CAR

After we leased our new Ford Escort, we set a goal of coming back to Ford in six months for a second car. Sharing a car can be a necessary burden, but for us it could work for only a short time.

In exactly six months we returned to the same Ford dealership. We knew exactly what we wanted. After we filled out a new credit application, Troy, our salesperson from before, made a call, and in less than five minutes were approved for our second car from Ford Motor Credit: a new black 1994 Ford Probe, with a radio.

Only six months of established credit allowed us this privilege. What next? My next goal was a new Mazda Miata.

OUR THIRD CAR

After our first two-year lease was up on the Ford Escort, we were in the new-car market again. It was time for the Mazda Miata. We knew by calling the lease sales manager that they didn't look favorably on bankruptcies, but we hoped our re-established credit, perfect payment history, and two excellent ratings with Ford would sway a lender in our favor. We also discovered that Ford Motor Credit owns Mazda Motor Credit.

After visiting a few Mazda dealerships and test-driving the car, we submitted our credit application to a dealer we thought could get the deal done. It was late in the evening, so we drove home with intentions of hearing something the following day. When we walked in the door there was a message from the dealer that Mazda Motor Credit had approved our lease. After wanting one for over two years, I was finally the owner of a new black 1995 Mazda Miata. We signed a three-year lease agreement. I loved it.

OUR FOURTH CAR

When our Ford Probe lease expired, my wife decided she wanted a Toyota Camry. We went to the same Toyota dealership that had turned us down three years earlier—the one that told us about the Ford dealer across the street. We were sloppy in handling this deal. We spoke with a car salesperson first. What a mess. It turned out that she was a new salesperson in training. I didn't have the heart to request an experienced salesperson, so I prepared for the worst. We were in the busy dealership two or three hours. At least I brought something to read. Always go through the new-car lease manager first.

Toyota Motor Credit approved us while we were still in the dealership. Had it not been for having leather installed in her car, my wife could have driven her new car home that night. My wife signed a three-year lease agreement with Toyota Motor Credit.

OUR FIFTH CAR

Three years is a long time to drive the same car. So we decided to sign only two-year leases. After being turned down by

Chrysler for a lease on a Cherokee Jeep Grand, the next day we returned to Ford Motor Credit in October 1997 to lease my wife a new 1998 Ford Explorer. No money down. Two-year lease. It has everything. That's what she wanted.

OUR SIXTH CAR

I was going through withdrawal not having a convertible just before the summer of 1998. I test drove a few different convertibles. Then I heard Mazda had redesigned the Miata, so I took the 1999 Miata out for a spin on a Saturday afternoon. By Monday, I leased a new 1999 dark blue Mazda Miata, with a CD player.

PRIDE

For those of you who have a hard time picturing yourself driving a Ford, you need to get over this. Sure, it may not be a Mercedes or BMW, but because you've chosen mainstream credit over other types of credit you will have many more choices for your next car.

My wife drove our first car off the dealership lot. Her first comment was, "I think they forgot something. This car doesn't have automatic locks. Can you call them tomorrow about it?" Yes, my wife has been spoiled. She assumed that every car has automatic locks.

Be thankful for the opportunity to start over again, and get over your pride. It will bring many rewards in the months and years to come. We're living proof of that.

IN CLOSING

The lesson here is to start slow and build up to what you want. After we had established excellent credit with Ford, other mainstream lenders were willing to lend to us as well. No one—except Ford—likes to be first in line.

25

How to Get Instant Credit

INSTANT CREDIT TODAY IS different than it used to be. In the old days, you showed a major bank card to a department store and within minutes were approved for "instant credit" with that store. Today there are very few true instant-credit programs offered. But a few still exist.

WHAT IS INSTANT CREDIT?

A real instant-credit program is where a customer can automatically qualify for credit using a major bank card as the only credit reference. And regardless of your credit history, you are approved, since they do not check your credit report.

Instant credit was really popular with department stores that issued their own credit cards in the 1980s. Their rationale was, if you could qualify for a major bank card, you would also be a good candidate for their card. And since you were such a good candidate, they didn't have to spend the time or money to check your credit. The major bank card company had already done that.

WHY IS INSTANT CREDIT IMPORTANT?

To someone who filed bankruptcy, instant credit is the second easiest way to re-establish unsecured credit. The first way is to reaffirm with companies included in your bankruptcy. As long as you don't overdo it, instant or reaffirmed credit will help put more positives on a negative credit report. The key is to not overdo it, and be very selective with which companies you choose. Our two were Sears and J.C. Penney. We reaffirmed with Sears and Lazarus. And J.C. Penney sent us a pre-approved card within a few months after closing on our mortgage.

HOW TO SPOT A FAKE

It's easy to spot a fake instant-credit program. Simply ask whether they review your credit report before issuing the card. If they do, it's a fake instant-credit program. If the salesclerk does not know for sure, do not accept his or her answer.

Most of the time you will need to ask for the telephone number of the credit department. Call them and ask a supervisor in the credit department to get the right answer. All you need to know is whether they review your credit application before granting credit.

WHAT MAKES A GOOD INSTANT-CREDIT PROGRAM

A real instant-credit program starts with knowledgeable sales associates who know the facts about the program. There is nothing more irritating than a sales associate who cannot get the facts straight. Unfortunately, this happens most of the time. If the sales associates in the store cannot answer your questions to your satisfaction, it's a good indication that they do not offer a real instant-credit program.

Next, you should be able to simply fill out a very short application, with no fine print at the bottom authorizing the company to review your credit report.

And finally, you should only need to present a major bank card. Any deviation from the above means that it's probably a fake instant-credit program.

PRE-APPROVED CREDIT VS. INSTANT CREDIT

Pre-approved credit is similar to instant credit, but different in two ways. For one thing, pre-approved credit usually comes to you in the mail. Second, you do not need to prove anything. The screening process has already been done.

Companies are always looking for creditworthy people to give their credit cards to. In fact, companies pay credit reporting agencies to pre-screen potential candidates for their credit cards. You see their inquiries on the bottom of your report. This type of inquiry does not hurt you, and is invisible to lenders who look at your credit report.

J.C. Penney is one of those companies. They look for new homeowners near one of their stores. Their philosophy is that if your credit is good enough to own a home, your credit is good enough to have one of their credit cards.

Three months after we closed on our house we received a pre-approved J.C. Penney credit-card application in the mail. I didn't believe it, so I read every word on the application. I then called the number on the application to confirm that it was real. It was true. All I needed to do was write my name, address, telephone number, and date of birth on the very short form and mail it back to J.C. Penney. No credit checks, no income verification, no nothing. Once they received it, I would become a cardholder in 10 days. And that's exactly what happened.

After using it for a few months, I asked for a card for my wife. That way its reporting on her credit reports as well.

The J.C. Penney's card was the only real pre-approved credit program I have seen first-hand in more than five years after bankruptcy. And it was a direct result of mortgaging our home.

AVOID TOO MUCH HIGH-INTEREST CREDIT

Do not wear yourself out trying to receive instant and pre-approved credit. This type of credit is usually very expensive, and should be used only sparingly. Do not to create a whole new wardrobe or transform your living area to an electronics wonder world. Keep these lines of credit open for when you *need* something.

Too much of this type of credit is a red flag to credit lenders that you have not changed your bad financial habits. It will hurt you. So consider it a blessing that you are unable to qualify for all the instant credit you think you deserve.

My wife and I carry only three department credit cards: J.C. Penney's, Sears, and a local department store, Lazarus. Sears and the local department store cards were reaffirmed after the bankruptcy.

The primary reason we use these cards are is household items, clothes, and gifts for other people. Things we need. Nothing else is allowed to be charged on those cards. As long as we pay the balance off each month, we do not mind having this type of credit. But for many people, it can be too tempting.

WHO GIVES INSTANT CREDIT?

The companies that still offer instant credit usually have one thing in common: They are usually the largest company in their industry. So if you need something, my advice would be to go to the largest national chain store nearest to you. Chances are they may have a instant credit program for you.

I do not believe in promoting instant credit. The use of too much easy credit led us into bankruptcy. So we steer clear as much as possible. Although there are companies that offer real instant-credit programs, we have mentioned only one such company here, to place emphasis on the importance of avoiding this type of credit.

LEVITZ FURNITURE

Levitz Furniture for many years used to be the place to go for instant credit to purchase furniture. You could walk in, present a major bank card, and within a few hours have new furniture. This has changed. As of January 1996 the company reverted to what they call "express credit." Express credit requires a review of your credit report before credit is granted.

Let me give you an idea of how the program has changed. We paid off our Levitz Furniture line of credit early. It was never late. In fact, we paid double payments for nearly one year.

We returned to Levitz Furniture after they changed their instant-credit program. We turned in an application and were promptly turned down for credit, due to the bankruptcy.

Keep in mind that we mortgaged a new home, had two major bank cards, bank loans, money in the bank, and paid off our previous account early. Go figure.

26

How to Get Other Credit

AS YOU BEGIN YOUR journey to re-establish credit after bankruptcy, there may be times when you are faced with the absolute need for credit for things other than the necessities (i.e., bank card, mortgage and car). Here are a few suggestions.

REAFFIRMED CREDIT

The easiest way to get other types of credit is to contact companies you had credit with before your bankruptcy and determine whether you would agree to pay what you owe if they would reactivate your account. Most of the time they will be more than willing to accommodate your request. It's in their best interest.

American Express does this. As long as you pay the debt back, they will consider reactivating the account.

Whatever you do, get everything in writing before you send anyone a check. If it's not in writing, it isn't a deal.

CELLULAR PHONE

Most cellular companies have rigid credit requirements. People with a previous bankruptcy who desire cellular service can purchase a cellular telephone outright, but are usually unable to get credit for the actual monthly service.

The few cellular companies that will approve credit with a previous bankruptcy demand a hefty security deposit, ranging from several hundred dollars to over one thousand dollars.

Cellular One, an aggressive cellular-service provider, developed a program for people unable to credit qualify. The program is called TalkBank. TalkBank will provide cellular service to people unable to qualify for credit, but with restrictions. You can make as many calls as you want in your cellular coverage range, but cannot make long-distance calls or calls while roaming unless they are billed to a credit card. The charges per minute tend to be a little higher than normal cellular service. In addition, TalkBank customers are limited to $125 a month. After their cellular bill reaches $125 each month, a payment will be required to continue service.

Call around to cellular providers in your area. Ask the office manager if there are programs you may qualify for with a previous bankruptcy. If you need cellular service, this is no time to beat around the bush. Ask specific questions to people who are in authority.

After you've had your limited cellular service for six months, call and ask when you will qualify for normal cellular service. This can save you a lot of money. My average cellular bill ranged from $75 to $100 a month. After I was approved to move into a normal cellular program, my average bill dropped to less than $40.

When I first called Cellular One I was told to wait 18 months before they could review the account for regular service. I called back and received a completely different answer. This time the other woman said I needed to wait six months. I called back again and a man told me that once I put in the request I would have an answer back in 24 hours. He showed up on my doorstep a few hours later with my new cellular phone. I had accomplished my goal: to receive normal cellular telephone service without having to pay a security deposit.

Another way is to apply for cellular service in your corporation's name. Don't have a corporation? Start one. Call the secretary of state's office in your state for instructions. Corporate filing fees usually range from $35 to $90. There are plenty of books at the library to help you fill the form out properly. If you have an accountant, they could also help with this.

Remember that you may not always be able to go through the front door in establishing credit after bankruptcy. Look for a window. If not a window, a back door. And with time, you will be able to walk through the front door.

LOCAL STORE CREDIT

I went to a seminar where the speaker made a statement that motivated me to action. He said, "...There are three things to leave behind when you pass on: your books, your journals, and your pictures..." It made me think. My wife and I didn't own a camera. I was suddenly inspired to go out and purchase a camera. And since I was up for the challenge, I decided I would purchase it on credit and pay it off in two months.

My search for credit to purchase a Nikon camera system began. I knew that my chances of being approved through normal channels were bleak, so I got creative. I remembered my father having a credit account with the local camera store when I was a kid. After making some initial calls to local camera stores, I decided the best way for me to get credit for a Nikon camera system was through a camera store that held its own credit accounts.

I began the project like any other, with lots of telephone calls and asking plenty of questions. I found a large camera store close to Indianapolis that had a reputation for working with professional photographers. After talking with a sales associate about the different types of financing for a camera, I quickly discerned that the credit programs by the camera manufacturers were not the best option, and in any case they were certainly the most expensive.

I then inquired about in-store credit with the ability to pay it off in two or three months. They faxed me a credit application. I was right: no fine print; no credit verification; and no review of my credit report. All they wanted to know was the names of a few companies I did business with, called trade references. Within a few days I was approved to purchase a Nikon camera system.

When looking for in-house credit, do not be too generous with information. My "sound bite" was that I wanted to avoid high interest. I did not say it was important that they not review my credit report. By looking at a credit application, it's easy to tell by reading the fine print just how far they go. If the fine print does not disclose that they will review your credit report, this is a good indication that this is the company you are looking for.

GASOLINE CARDS

One of the major gasoline companies offers its credit card to people with a bankruptcy. Citgo is pretty lenient, but will not extend credit to people with unpaid tax liens or tax levies. Once these are paid, and you meet their other basic qualifications, chances are good you will be approved for their gas card. For more information, call (800) GO CITGO.

We ended up going with Shell. They have easy requirements to obtain a corporate card. We filled out the corporate fleet card application and were promptly mailed two Shell gas cards. The key is to have a corporation. You can pick-up an application in most Shell stations or call (800) 377-5150. Ask for the Shell Fleet Card application to be mailed to your corporation.

There's another way to get a gas card. It takes a little longer, and involves purchasing stock in the company. I've known people who received a gas card using this method. Contact me for more information.

HEAT PUMPS AND WATER SOFTENERS

It is easier to get approved for this type of thing if you go through the company offering the product. They have more leverage than going directly to the bank on your own. Few of these programs are funded by banks, and those are the best ones. Steer clear of programs offered by finance companies or bancs. Not only does a finance-company credit reference weaken your credit report, but the interest rate is also too high.

Your next option is to find a small company that will extend credit to you. That's what we did when our heat pump went out. We talked with the owner, and he agreed to put in our heat pump based on a payment plan we mutually agreed upon.

Sometimes you have to get creative. Don't be afraid to ask.

27

How to Increase
Your Credit Limits

ONCE YOU HAVE ESTABLISHED credit with a company, it's important to keep increasing your credit limit. While this may not be practical for an auto loan or home mortgage, it certainly applies for bank cards, department store credit, and other types of revolving credit. Every six months, call to request an increase.

WHY BOTHER TO INCREASE YOUR LIMIT?

Raising your limit is important. The larger the amount a lender is willing to trust you with, the more it may influence another lender to grant you a similar line of credit.

A credit lender looks at several things to evaluate your creditworthiness. For example, let's say you have a Visa bank card with a $300 line of credit. You've paid on time for 6 to 12 months. Your car breaks down and you need to repair it fast. The auto mechanic gives you an estimate of $1,000. But no bank will extend you $1,000 credit to repair your car. By taking the time to raise your credit limit over a period of time, this emergency could have been covered.

Sure, you will reach a point where higher limits are of no significance to you. But until then, keep raising them. You'll be glad you did.

HOW TO INCREASE YOUR LIMIT

All you need to do is ask. Simply call the lender's customer assistance department and request a credit-limit increase. That's all there is to it.

The only time not to do this is with credit cards you did not file bankruptcy on. Never ask for a credit-limit increase on these cards. Let it happen automatically. You run the risk of the company canceling your credit card once they know you bankruptcy.

Most companies review credit limits every six months. Make it a habit to call for a credit-limit increase every six months. Write it in your day planner so you don't forget.

You may experience the joy of talking with customer service people who do not understand the meaning of providing customer service. They may tell you they don't know when your limit will be raised. Or that it happens automatically. In this case, simply ask when was the last time the credit limit was increased, and cheerfully end the call. Immediately mark in your day planner to call back six months from that date to request a credit increase.

And don't ask for any specific amount of increase. Let them decide the amount.

THE RIGHT TO ASK

You are entitled to ask for a credit-limit increase only if you have paid your monthly payments early or on time. Timely payments are what the lender is looking for, and they will determine whether your request is approved.

IMPROVE YOUR CHANCES

Most stores will be more eager to grant your request if you are either calling from the store ready to make the purchase or you request an increase during the busiest season—the Christmas holiday. Be careful though, you run the risk of being embarrassed if you are turned down at the register. I prefer using the telephone in the store's credit department, or calling from home.

DON'T TAKE NO FOR AN ANSWER

If you've done all the right things, and they still say no, ask to speak to a supervisor. This happened to us with both of our

Orchard Bank bank cards. Both were at a $2,000 credit limit. I asked for an increase. They turned us down. I asked to speak to a supervisor. Both credit limits were raised to $2,500 and the interest rate was even lowered by 4%.

If you've done all the right things, don't take no for an answer. Politely ask to speak to a supervisor.

28

Standing Up to the IRS

WHERE THERE IS SMOKE, there is fire. Where there is a bankruptcy, there are usually unresolved problems with the IRS. Dealing with the IRS can seem intimidating. It doesn't have to be. With the proper advice, a whole new world of options can be brought to your attention.

The key to improved relations with the IRS is either becoming a tax expert yourself or else locating a person experienced in handling these matters for you.

Do not take the threat of tax liens and levies lightly. You need to avoid federal tax liens and levies at all costs. They not only temporarily damage your credit report, but they also may put you in a holding pattern stopping you from obtaining new credit until the liens are paid or subordinated. In our case, tax liens forced us to wait before we could mortgage a larger home. However, in some situations, with a signed installment agreement with the IRS and a 12-month payment history, mortgage companies can still close the deal.

The goal of this chapter is to lead you to professionals who can help you resolve your tax problem. For a complete understanding on the topic of working with the IRS, I recommend reading: *"Stand Up to the IRS"* by Frederick W. Daily. Be sure to request the most recent version, since it is frequently updated to stay current with tax law.

IT HAPPENED TO US

Within three weeks of receiving a letter from the IRS stating their intent to levy on us, it happened.

My wife called from her cellular phone. In tears, she shouted at me, explaining that 100% of her next paycheck was going to be levied by the IRS.

The IRS had officially garnished her wages. She was very embarrassed and worried that we would not be able to make ends meet. Fortunately, we had previously taken steps to ensure that the IRS would be limited in what they could do, if in fact there ever was a levy against our wages.

The good news: Days before her next paycheck, we had a signed release of the lien and a $50-a-month installment agreement with the IRS on an alleged $188,000 debt.

If we hadn't had a tax professional waiting in the wings, we might have become the latest victims of an unfair IRS tax levy. Before you do anything else, be sure to get your tax professional working on your case. Do not let any excuses hold you back. Because when the IRS moves, it moves. And you must be ready.

MY MISTAKE

I was always successful in buying extra time with the IRS. But the mistake I made was to neglect to do anything constructive, like finding someone to help me after I bought the time. I always procrastinated in taking the time to find quality help.

What triggered our levy was my failure to call back the IRS at a specific time to update them on our situation. I had written the call-back day on the wrong month in my day planner!

The best thing to do is to seek competent, specialized help from people who have a background in working with the IRS, as early in the process as possible. Our entire levy could have been avoided if I had found our tax pro earlier.

TAX PROS

There are professionals who specialize in helping people with tax problems. They are known as tax pros. They understand what the IRS wants, and they can represent you or give you advice on how you can represent yourself. Some tax pros use to work with the IRS. As in any other profession, there are good tax pros and bad ones. A good one is worth his or her weight in gold.

Tax pros come in three flavors. You can choose an:

1.   Enrolled agent
2.   Tax attorney
3.   Certified Public Accountant

ENROLLED AGENTS (EA)

An EA is usually a full-time tax advisor and tax preparer who is permitted to practice before the IRS in all matters. Most EAs cannot represent you in tax court, however. They earn the designation "enrolled agent" by either passing a difficult exam or having at least five years of experience working for the IRS. They also must participate in continuing education programs to retain their EA designations.

There are approximately 34,000 EAs in the United States, 9,200 of whom are members of the National Association of Enrolled Agents. EAs are usually the least expensive of all tax pros. For a cost-effective approach to handling a tax problem, or if your tax problem involves less than $10,000, consider an EA.

A lot of EAs I've met around the country use to work for the IRS. There's something about these individuals that compels your trust. All former IRS employees I've met are very experienced EAs. I would hire any of them to handle a tax matter under $10,000.

What you need to watch out for is former IRS employees who are still loyal to the IRS. I've seen it first-hand. One of our seminar tax pro sponsors in Cleveland carried the IRS tax code around like some folks carry their Bible. Very competent fellow. Highly knowledgeable in the tax code. But would he fight for me, and present my case in the best light? That's the question you must ask yourself.

TAX ATTORNEYS

Tax attorneys are lawyers who do various types of tax-related work, including complex tax and estate planning, IRS dispute resolution, and sometimes tax-return preparation. To assure competence, look for a tax attorney with either a special tax-law degree or a certification as a tax-law specialist from a state bar association. If more than $10,000 is at stake, or the IRS is accusing you of committing fraud, or you're headed to tax court, call a tax attorney.

We've met a few tax attorneys. I think they have what it takes to represent you well. They have the balance of knowledge and sales skills to present your case. The downside in using a tax attorney is the cost. Here in Indianapolis, it's five times the cost of using an enrolled agent. If your IRS debt is over $100,000, I would recommend working strictly with a tax attorney.

I've found a tax attorney that really understands his business. His name is Larry Heinkel. He's a tax attorney that understands bankruptcy and tax issues on a national basis. You can reach him at (407) 426-9009 In meeting a new tax pro every weekend for nearly two years, I trust you're in good hands.

CERTIFIED PUBLIC ACCOUNTANTS (CPAs)

CPAs are licensed and regulated in all states. They do sophisticated accounting and business audit work, and prepare tax returns. To become a CPA, an accountant must have a college degree and work experience with a CPA firm, and must pass a series of rigorous examinations. Some CPAs have a great deal of IRS experience, but many do little IRS work. Of those who do, many are as good as tax attorneys and charge about the same or even a little less. Some CPAs, however, are not as aggressive as tax lawyers when facing the IRS personnel.

HOW A TAX PRO CAN HELP

Most auditors and collectors prefer dealing with experienced tax pros. It makes their job easier. Good tax pros know what the IRS wants, and they don't waste time.

If you face an audit, collection of a tax bill or a tax court hearing, and you've decided to at least consult a tax pro, here are the ways an experienced tax pro can help:

Consultation and advice: A tax pro can analyze your situation and advise you on the best plan of action. Rarely is there only one way to handle an IRS matter. He or she should describe your alternatives so you can make an informed choice.

Negotiation: Tax pros often possess negotiating skills. And an experienced tax pro should know what kinds of deals can't be made with the IRS.

Representation: Experienced tax pros know IRS procedures and how to maneuver around the IRS bureaucracy. Tax pros can neutralize the intimidation factor that the IRS knows it holds over you. And if you have something to hide, a tax pro usually can keep the lid on it better than you can.

DO YOU NEED HELP?

Under the taxpayer's Bill of Rights you have the right to have a representative handle any IRS matter for you. This means you never have to face the IRS if you don't want to.

In general, you can safely go it alone in the two most common, but serious, IRS situations:

- You are being audited and your records are in order, you can substantiate everything on your return and you have nothing to hide, or

- The IRS is seeking to collect an overdue tax bill of $10,000 or less and you can pay it off within 36 months.

But before making any decision on proceeding alone or with a tax pro, weigh the pros and cons of each.

GOING-IT-ALONE ANALYSIS

Pro: You save professional fees.

Con: It takes a lot of time.
You may find it very stressful.
You may say or do the wrong thing.

CONSULTING A TAX PRO BEFORE FACING THE IRS

Pro: You get the information you need, and gain

confidence. It's cheaper than hiring a tax pro to represent you.

Con: Most tax pros charge for consultation.

HIRING A TAX PRO TO REPRESENT YOU

Pro: The IRS respects knowledgeable tax pros
You don't face the IRS.
Tax pros know tax issues.

Con: Tax pros are expensive if they are good.
You understand your tax records best.
You lose some control over your case, and risk hiring someone who is inexperienced or incompetent.

WHERE TO FIND A TAX PRO

There are several ways to find a good tax pro. Asking the IRS is not one of them. Here are some practical ways to find the right tax pro for you:

Ask your tax advisor or accountant. They might have a good recommendation of a tax pro who can help you deal with an IRS problem.

Look in the Yellow Pages under "Tax Consultants & Representatives." Most tax pros offer a first consultation by phone or in their office at no charge. Look for the words "enrolled agent" or "licensed to practice before the IRS." Some tax pros boldly state in their advertising they use to work for the IRS.

Ask experienced Realtors. These people deal with all sorts of financial situations every day. Good ones know a lot of people.

Professional associations and referral panels. Most local bar associations will give out the names of tax attorneys who practice in your area. But bar associations don't meaningfully screen the attorneys listed. Those who are listed may not be experienced or competent.

To find an EA in your area, call the National Association of Enrolled Agents at (800) 424-4339 or (301) 984-6232. To find a CPA, try calling a local or state CPA society.

WHAT TO LOOK FOR IN A TAX PRO

Once you have the name of a tax pro, call and ask to speak with him or her directly. If the person is too busy to talk to you—and your call isn't transferred to another tax specialist—assume that the office is too busy to handle your case, and call the next person on your list.

When you speak to a tax pro, try to develop rapport. Mention how you got his name, especially if it was a personal referral. Then get to the point: Tell him your tax problem. If he doesn't handle your type of situation, ask for the names of some people who do. Here are some other suggestions for making a good match:

- Don't be in a hurry to hire the first tax pro you speak to. It took over 13 months to find ours. Your decision is important, and rarely is there only one person for the job. Talk to a few. Choose the one you communicate with best. Ask to speak to a few recent customers.

- Question the tax pro carefully about his IRS experience. No matter how well he or she knows the tax code, prior IRS dealings are key. Previous IRS employment is not always a plus. It may have forever impressed the IRS point of view on him. Also, be skeptical if he hasn't been in practice at least five years.

- Does the tax pro seem to be aggressive or timid in discussing your case? If he seems awed by the IRS, find someone else.

- Does the tax pro give you a feeling of confidence? Ask him the likely outcome of your case. While no one can predict the future, his answer should create trust. Look for an honest response, not necessarily a rosy picture.

If you lose faith in your tax pro, find another one fast. But don't dismiss the first one until you get a second opinion on what he is doing. And don't fire a tax pro simply because nothing is happening. Frequently, inaction is because the IRS is dragging its feet. Remember, delay often works to your advantage in dealing with the IRS.

TAX PRO FEES

Be sure to get an understanding about the tax pro's fees at your first meeting. Does he charge by the hour or work by a flat fee? Most professionals charge $25 to $250 per hour, depending on where you live, the type of case, and exactly what you want the tax pro to do. Our tax pro charged us a flat fee of $2,000.

To some extent, you can control costs. Tax pros can be either hired as consultants, meaning you handle you own case and ask for advice as needed, or hired to represent you from start to finish. In other words, going to a tax pro need not be an all-or-nothing affair.

Although uncertainty about costs leaves most folks uncomfortable, many good tax pros shy away from quoting flat fees. When they do, it's usually for straightforward matters. But even if the tax pro won't give you a firm estimate, he should be able to "ballpark" a range of hours necessary for your case.

Most tax pros require a retainer paid in advance, often equal to the minimum time estimated as needed on the case.

TIPS ON CONTROLLING A TAX PRO'S FEES

- If you like the tax pro but not his fee, ask whether he can do it for less. If he isn't very busy, he may be flexible on fee and payment arrangements. Small tax firms or solo practitioners are more likely than professionals in large offices to negotiate the fee.
- Consider asking for a written fee agreement and monthly billings with itemized statements of time and services

rendered. This will keep the tax pro honest. In many states, attorneys are required to give you a written fee agreement before starting work.

- If you disagree with a bill you receive, call your tax pro. If the firm is interested in retaining your business, he should listen to your concerns, adjust the bill, or work to satisfy you. If the tax pro won't budge, call your state or local CPA society or your state's bar association. Many groups have panels that help professionals and clients mediate fee disputes.

29

What We Learned in Dealing with the IRS

WHEN IT COMES TO paying the IRS the taxes you owe, you really have four options.

Pay in full. An obvious choice.

Pay a monthly installment agreement. Nearly one million Americans are on an installment agreement with the IRS each year. I wouldn't recommend doing it yourself unless you are a master negotiator or do significant reading on the subject. Otherwise, hire a tax pro. They know what the IRS wants and can negotiate the best deal for you. My tax pro negotiated a $50 monthly installment agreement on an alleged $88,000 tax bill, with an understanding that an offer in compromise was forthcoming.

Reduce, eliminate or pay debt through bankruptcy. Bankruptcy can possibly reduce your total tax liability. Not so much the tax itself, but the penalties and interest. Very rarely are taxes completely eliminated. If bankruptcy attorneys were more savvy at knowing the rules, more people might qualify.

If my wife and I had waited two more months, the majority of our tax bill would have been dischargeable. A Chapter 13 bankruptcy can be strategically used to force the IRS into a payment agreement you can afford, even if you have already filed Chapter 7. Talk with a tax pro.

Offer in compromise. This is where you basically say to the IRS that you can afford to pay them X-amount of dollars to resolve your tax bill. *The amount you accept has nothing to do with the amount you owe, and has everything to do with the amount of assets you have.*

Our revised edition of this book will have more information on this subject, since we have just submitted our offer in compromise to the IRS. In the meantime, for more information on this subject see the books mentioned at the beginning of this chapter.

SEIZURE POWER

The IRS has far greater powers than any other bill collector. The agency has the power to take your wages, bank accounts and other property without even first granting you a hearing. You should be successful in buying time, but don't rest on your success. It's only temporary. The sooner you develop a strategy, the sounder you will sleep at night.

THE "AUTOMATIC STAY"

The beauty of the "automatic stay" is that the moment you filed your bankruptcy petition, virtually all your creditors were stopped in their tracks. The automatic stay even prevents federal and state tax collectors from seizing your property and issuing lien notices—for a period of time. There are restrictions, however.

The automatic stay does not stop a tax audit, the issuance of a tax deficiency notice, a demand for a tax return, the issuance of a tax assessment, or the demand for payment of such an assessment. In addition, some types of debts cannot be erased in Chapter 7 bankruptcy:

1. Certain tax debts
2. Recent student loans
3. Child support
4. Debts incurred by fraud

The issues surrounding the discharging of debts listed above are very technical. A tax professional should be retained for a complete and thorough understanding as to how it applies to you.

The bottom line is that the rules for discharging penalties and interest are less stringent than for discharging the underlying taxes.

SUSPENDING YOUR TAX BILL

If your finances are bleak (what better reason than bankruptcy?) and you have no job, little or no money, and no immediate prospects, you can ask a revenue officer or other IRS collector to "53" your case. If he or she agrees, it means that he recommends to his supervisors that your tax account balance be deemed "currently not collectable."

Once your account have been declared a "53," you won't hear from the IRS concerning your tax bill for up to one year. The IRS stops bothering you, but interest (and sometimes penalties) still accrue. At the end of your "53" period, the computer brings your account back up and you start the process over again.

The IRS doesn't take the "53" procedure lightly. You must persuade the IRS that you are almost destitute—that even a $25-a-month installment agreement is beyond your means.

Having your case classified as "currently not collectable" doesn't really solve your tax problem. It does, however, let you delay dealing with it. The "53" process simply buys time.

OTHER WAYS TO BUY TIME

Simply tell the IRS that you filed bankruptcy and need time to get back on your feet. If you don't have a job, tell them. Tell them anything truthful to buy time.

Question the accuracy of your tax bill. If there is ever a question about the accuracy of the tax bill, it should be an automatic extension of more time.

File an amended return. Filing amended returns is evidence that there may be a question of the accuracy of the tax bill. This helps the delay process.

Submit an offer in compromise. Once your offer is submitted, the IRS usually does not harass you if it's a legitimate offer. Offers in compromise take anywhere to four to 12 months to get accepted.

I was very concerned about having anything negative show up on my credit report. I told the collection officers that I felt I might be able to get a loan after two years. Telling them this not only bought me time, but also prevented tax liens from posting to my credit report for a time. It wasn't until I dropped the ball in communicating with the IRS that the bottom fell out of my strategy. From that point on, tax liens were reported to the credit reporting agencies.

BEFORE YOU SPEAK WITH A TAX COLLECTOR

Never lie to the IRS. It's a crime.

Become a tax pro, or hire one fast. If you don't have a tax pro yet, and a tax collector calls, tell him that you are in the process of retaining a tax professional and would like to reschedule this conversation. Then proceed to arrange a time for your tax pro to call the collector back and or give the tax collector your tax pro's name and telephone number.

Have an action plan. If you don't have a plan, the IRS will. You can develop an action plan by reading the books mentioned at the beginning of this chapter on this subject, or hiring a tax pro to advise you.

Avoid information about bank accounts and other assets. We always gave the IRS bank-account information on accounts we hardly ever used. If they persist, a technique that has been used effectively is the "disconnected" technique. Simply hang up the telephone in the middle of a sentence. Your next call should be to your tax pro, so they get a busy signal when they call back.

Communicate. People who hide from the IRS will some day be sorry they did. It's so much easier to communicate. You're a fool if you tell them too much, though. It's like playing poker and showing your opponents your cards.

Use a day planner to keep track of dates and conversations. It is very important to remember your call-back dates with the IRS. If you miss one of these dates, their computer will automatically proceed to the next step. If you don't own a day planner, run to your nearest Franklin Quest store and pick one up.

WHAT IS A TAX LIEN?

A tax lien is a notice to the world that you owe taxes. The IRS cannot collect any money by just filing a tax lien. If the IRS sends you a tax bill and you don't contest or pay it, the IRS has a right to inform the public that you owe taxes. This is done by recording a Notice of Federal Tax Lien at your county recorder's office (where real estate transactions are recorded).

The practical effect of a tax lien is to scare off potential lenders or buyers and to warn others that you are a tax deadbeat. The tax lien notice will be picked up by credit reporting agencies such as Experian, Equifax and Trans Union.

Tax liens are not easily removed once recorded, unless you pay the taxes, penalties and interest in full.

WHAT IS A TAX LEVY?

A tax levy is how the IRS must seize your property—by way of levy—to collect what you owe. Usually this means taking money held from you by others, such as your bank, stockbroker or employer.

Before the IRS seizes your money or property, you must be sent a Notice of Intent to Levy. This gives you 30 days from the date of the notice to pay in full what you owe. The law requires only that the IRS send the notice—not that you actually receive it.

If you are unemployed, have only the clothes on your back and no money in the bank, you are a poor levy target for the IRS. If and when your financial situation improves, you'll have to worry about the IRS property-seizure power.

WHAT IS AN OFFER IN COMPROMISE?

An offer in compromise is a one-page written proposal to the IRS that basically proves you are unable to pay the debt, but are willing to pay a fixed amount either in one lump sum or over time, then call it even.

These offers are very common, and are usually handled by a tax pro on your behalf. The problem is that they can take from four to 12 months to get approved. They are handled on a case-by-case basis, so there is no typical deal. Everything varies, based on the facts surrounding each individual's situation.

Offers in compromise have nothing to do with the amount of taxes owed, but they have everything to do with your ability to pay.

The IRS accepted our office in compromise on June 7, 1999. An on an alleged debt of $188,000 they took $8,250 as payment in full. Is the IRS accepting more and more offers? Yes. Would I submit an offer on my own? No. I highly recommend hiring a tax pro to fill-out the paperwork and negotiate on your behalf.

Here are the three best tax pros I know:

Judy Summit   (317) 842-3677
Steve Maese   (415) 457-0202
Larry Heinkel   (407) 426-9009

30

Action Plans

THIS BOOK IS DESIGNED to help people who have already filed bankruptcy. Here is some parting advice for people at various stages of their bankruptcy.

RECENTLY FILED

If you recently filed bankruptcy, you need to immediately do the following:

1. *Reduce your cost of living.* Terminate cable television, cancel newspaper delivery, stop eating out, write letters instead of making long-distance telephone calls, disconnect your car phone, avoid using credit cards for a time, purchase fewer groceries, sell anything you no longer need, and return things you haven't used for credit.

2. *Improve your income.* Move where the jobs are. Work somewhere in a neighboring city. Call headhunters (if you have access to the internet, log onto *www.headhunter.net* and job placement services. Read *"The New Quick Job-Hunting Map"* by Richard Nelson Bolles. Update your résumé using the dictionary of skill synonyms or related words toward the back of the book.

3. *Give.* You must learn to give. Giving comes before saving. Educated people know that giving starts the receiving process. Start with 10% of your income. It's a

ancient principle. If you don't know where to give, find
a local church and plant it there. If a church is out of the
question right now, find a non-profit entity you could
support. Giving will radically change your life.

4.   *Pay on time.* Don't even think about being late on any
      credit that reports to the credit reporting agencies. After
      bankruptcy, people will judge you on your payment
      history after bankruptcy. You've been given a second
      chance, so take advantage of it.

5.   *Goals.* Write on a piece of paper a summary of where
      you are and what's happening in your life right now. On
      another piece of paper, talk about where you want to be
      in three months, six months, and 12 months from now.
      Answer questions like: Where do you want to live? What
      type of work would you most enjoy? How much money
      do you want to earn? What type of car do you want to
      drive? Write as much as you can. It may help to use this
      question: "If I could have anything I wanted, what would
      it be, and why?"

6.   *Save money.* Do whatever it takes to save as much
      money as you can. Appoint whoever is best at handling
      the money to manage it. Maybe your spouse? The more
      savings you have, the more options you will have. It's
      that simple. Start by saving 10% of every dollar you
      earn. More, if you can.

7.   *Mainstream credit.* You may begin to receive many
      offers in the mail from companies that say they want to
      help you establish credit. Find a shoebox and place all
      these mailings in the box, then forget about them. Read
      the chapter on understanding the difference between
      "mainstream credit" and "other credit." The difference
      will mean recovering in months versus years.

8.   Read chapter one personal development once a month

for a year.

PREVIOUSLY FILED

Follow all the above as well as:

9.   *Credit reports.* Obtain a copy of your credit reports to make sure that current credit liabilities reporting to the credit reporting agencies are accurate. You cannot afford wrong information.

10. *Other credit.* If you have any "other credit," plan to get rid of it as soon as possible. This type of credit will hurt you more than you realize.

THINKING ABOUT FILING

You need to speak with an attorney specializing in bankruptcy as soon as possible to determine what your options are. The Yellow Pages will help you find a qualified attorney. Here are some things to look for in an attorney:

1.   *Must specialize in bankruptcy.* Although there are good attorneys who do more than bankruptcy, you're better off with an attorney who does bankruptcy proceedings every day. Especially if you choose to file a Chapter 13 bankruptcy.

2.   *If your attorney is determined that you file Chapter 13 bankruptcy protection, get a second opinion.* I personally believe most people are better off filing Chapter 7. My reasons are based on statistics. The majority of the people who file Chapter 13 bankruptcy convert to Chapter 7 within the first year. You end up paying double attorney fees. Whether you file Chapter 7 or 13, it affects you the same. There are no Brownie points for filing Chapter 13. In fact, you're penalized for three to five years. My recommendation would be to file Chapter 7 bankruptcy, and consider working out a payment plan

with your creditors on your own terms.

3.   *Payment plans.* No bankruptcy attorney I know will
     allow you to pay as you go. Ask about the payment
     policy. If you don't get the answer you want, ask the
     attorney directly during your initial conversation. We
     offered to do a lot of the work ourselves, and saved a lot
     of money.

PREVIOUS BANKRUPTCY AND LIVING ON CASH-ONLY BASIS

The most important thing for you to understand is that you need
to develop a credit history after bankruptcy before lenders will
work with you. Without a recent payment history, they have no
way of determining whether you are financially responsible.
Living on a cash-only system is a good thing. I recommend it.
But if you don't get back into the credit system, you will need
cash to pay for everything now and in the future. If you won't do
it for yourself, do it for your children. What are you going to say
when your kids come to you for help in buying their first car or
first home? Re-established some credit, then go back to your
cash-only system.

PREVIOUS BANKRUPTCY AND HEADING FOR A SECOND ONE

I've worked with people first-hand in this situation. It's ugly.
They never changed their habits. Even the coach of the
Washington Redskins filed bankruptcy twice. In order for this
book to help you, it's important to realize that your way is not
working. It's time you bought into someone else's plan. Focus on
drastically reducing your cost of living and increasing your
income. Ignore all types of credit for six months. Learn to live on
a cash-only system.

I would also encourage you to seek a spiritual foundation. A
great place to start is with Bible Study Fellowship International,
or BSF for short. BSF is an international, non-denominational,
non-profit organization. They offer free classes in over 950 cities

around the world. For information about BSF call their headquarters at (210) 492-4676. You'll be glad you did. Access their web site at: *www.bsfinternational.org*

TWICE BANKRUPT

Although there may be some cases that are excusable, like medical or layoffs, having filed twice is usually a sign of internal problems that need to be resolved quickly.

How to Contact the Author

I would love hearing from you. I enjoy reading letters, e-mail messages, and faxes. Please feel free to contact me using any of the following ways.

E-mail:	stephen@afterbankruptcy.com
Fax:	(317) 578-8747
By letter:	AB Foundation, Inc. c/o Stephen Snyder 6520 Wandsworth Circle Indianapolis, Indiana 46250-3410 USA
Office:	(317) 578-7118

Share Your Success

Let me encourage you to share your success. What have you done after bankruptcy? Please let me know. As an incentive, my publisher will send you a copy of my second favorite book, *"Success: The Glenn Bland Method,"* for your written response.

Testimony

I FILED BANKRUPTCY WHEN I was a Christian. I knew about God, but I didn't know God. There is a big difference.

I'm convinced that my success was and is a direct result of following His ways, as illustrated in the pages of our instruction manual—The Bible.

One of His instructions is the principle of giving God the first 10 percent of whatever you earn. This was very hard for me. I finally came to the realization that my way wasn't working, and it would be wise to listen to someone else's plan.

Let me tell you that ever since my wife and I put God first in our lives with our money, everything changed. I would encourage you to do the same. Find a local church and plant your giving there. Be sure to give cheerfully, and base your giving on His promises, which you will find in the Bible.

I believe Jesus Christ is the Son of God, was crucified, died, and on the third day rose again. And now sits on the right-hand of God the Father. His Holy Spirit lives in me and in all true believers.

In closing, you do not need to be a Christian to use this book. But, I believe that having God on your side is the best possible partnership anyone could have.

Most people do not know that the only prayer God answers from people who do not know Him is a prayer to ask Him to come into their hearts. Please consider asking Him into your life today. For more information, call (317) 578-7118 or write me personally.

If you are interested in learning more about what the Bible says about practical everyday living, I encourage you to call Bible Study Fellowship, commonly known as BSF. BSF is a worldwide Bible study organization that can be called the Mercedes Benz of Bible studies. It's free. And there's a local group that meets near you. The entire world is learning the same lesson every week. So if you travel a lot, you can always find a local meeting. Our group in Indianapolis is one of the largest, with nearly 600 men meeting every Monday for two hours. There are women's groups too.

This Bible study group helped do what few churches have done for me: Take me from a part-time Christian to an active Christian. Call BSF headquarters and ask for the nearest BSF men's or women's group nearest you. Call (888) 273-2527.

The greatest single cause of atheism in the world today is other Christians who say it with their mouths and deny it with their lifestyles.

My best friend was born in a manger.

STEPHEN SNYDER

Stephen Snyder
September 1998

"Life changes only when you act upon what you learn."
—Stephen Snyder

Appendix A

The following is a partial list of State Housing Authorities around the country. Call to inquire about special first-time homebuyer programs, or programs to help you with your down payment.

Theresa Parker, Executive Director
California Housing Finance Agency
1121 L Street, 7th Floor
Sacramento, CA 95814
916/322-3991   Fax: 916/324-8640

David W. Herlinger, Executive Director
Colorado Housing and Finance Authority
1981 Blake Street
Denver, CO 80202-1272
303/297-2432   Fax: 303/297-2615

Susan J. Leigh, Chief Executive Officer and Board Secretary
Florida Housing Finance Corporation
227 North Bronough Street, Suite 5000
Tallahassee, FL 32301-1329
904/488-4197   Fax: 904/488-9809

David B. Pinson, Director, Housing Finance
Georgia Department of Community Affairs/Georgia HFA
60 Executive Parkway South
Atlanta, GA 30329
404/679-4840   Fax: 404/679-4844

Jim Higdon, Commissioner
Georgia Department of Community Affairs/Georgia Housing and Finance Authority
60 Executive Parkway South, Suite 250
Atlanta, GA 30329
404/679-4840   Fax: 404/679-4837

John N. Varones, Executive Director
Illinois Housing Development Authority
401 North Michigan Avenue, Suite 900
Chicago, IL 60611
312/836-5200   Fax: 312/832-2170

Robert V. Welch Jr., Executive Director
Indiana Housing Finance Authority
115 West Washington Street
National City Center, South Tower, Suite 1350
Indianapolis, IN 46204
317/232-7777   Fax: 317/232-7778

F. Lynn Luallen, Chief Executive Officer
Kentucky Housing Corporation
1231 Louisville Road
Frankfort, KY 40601
502/564-7630   Fax: 502/564-7322

James L. Logue III, Executive Director
Michigan State Housing Development Authority
Plaza One Building, Fifth Floor
401 South Washington Square
Lansing, MI 48933
517/373-8370   Fax: 517/335-4797

Katherine G. Hadley, Commissioner
Minnesota Housing Finance Agency
400 Sibley Street, Suite 300
St. Paul, MN 55101
612/296-7608   Fax: 612/296-8139

Richard G. Grose, Executive Director
Missouri Housing Development Commission
3435 Broadway
Kansas City, MO 64111
816/759-6600 Fax: 816/759-6828

Charles L. Horsey III, Administrator
Nevada Housing Division
1802 North Carson, Suite 154
Carson City, NV 89701
702/687-4258 Fax: 702/687-4040

Timothy Touhey, Executive Director
New Jersey Housing and Mortgage Finance Agency
637 South Clinton Avenue
P.O. Box 18550
Trenton, NJ 08650-2085
609/278-7400 Fax: 609/278-1754

Barbara Udell, President
New York City Housing Development Corporation
75 Maiden Lane, 8th Floor
New York, NY 10038
212/344-8080 Fax: 212/269-6121

Joseph B. Lynch, Acting Commissioner
New York State Division of Housing and Community Renewal
Hampton Plaza
38-40 State Street
Albany, NY 12207
518/486-3370 Fax: 518/473-9462

Stephen J. Hunt, President/CEO
New York State Housing Finance Agency/State of New York Mortgage Agency
641 Lexington Avenue
New York, NY 10022
212/688-4000 Fax: 212/872-0301

Richard Everhart, Executive Director
Ohio Housing Finance Agency
77 South High Street, 26th Floor
Columbus, OH 43215-6108
614/466-7970   Fax: 614/644-5393

Dennis Shockley, Executive Director
Oklahoma Housing Finance Agency
1140 Northwest 63rd, Suite 200
Oklahoma City, OK 73116
405/848-1144   Fax: 405/840-1109

Bob Repine, Director
Oregon Housing and Community Services Department
1600 State Street
Salem, OR 97310-0302
503/986-2000   Fax: 503/986-2020

William C. Bostic, Executive Director
Pennsylvania Housing Finance Agency
P.O. Box 8029
Harrisburg, PA 17105-8029
717/780-3800   Fax: 717/780-3905

W. Jeff Reynolds, Executive Director
Tennessee Housing Development Agency
404 James Robertson Parkway, Suite 1114
Nashville, TN 37243-0900
615/741-2400   Fax: 615/741-9634

Larry Paul Manley, Executive Director
Texas Department of Housing and Community Affairs
P.O. Box 13941
Austin, TX 78711-3941
512/475-3800   Fax: 512/469-9606

William H. Erickson, Executive Director
Utah Housing Finance Agency
554 South 300 East
Salt Lake City, UT 84111
801/521-6950   Fax: 801/323-2660

John Ritchie Jr., Executive Director
Virginia Housing Development Authority
601 South Belvidere Street
Richmond, VA 23220-6504
804/782-1986   Fax: 804/783-6704

Kim Herman, Executive Director
Washington State Housing Finance Commission
1000 Second Avenue, Suite 2700
Seattle, WA 98104-1046
206/464-7139   Fax: 206/587-5113

Fritz Ruf, Executive Director
Wisconsin Housing and Economic Development Authority
P.O. Box 1728
Madison, WI 53701-1728
608/266-7884   Fax: 608/267-1099

If your state is not listed above call After Bankruptcy Foundation for the telephone number of the nearest location nearest you.

For more information:

After Bankruptcy Foundation, Inc.
6520 Wandsworth Circle
Indianapolis, Indiana 46250-3410
Phone: (317) 578-7118
Fax: (317) 578-8747
email: stephen@afterbankruptcy.com
Web site: www.afterbankruptcy.org

"If you can believe, all things are possible to him who believes"—Mark 9:23